PROPERTIUS:
A CRITICAL INTRODUCTION

PROPERTIUS

A CRITICAL INTRODUCTION

J. P. SULLIVAN

Faculty Professor of Arts and Letters
State University of New York
at Buffalo

CAMBRIDGE UNIVERSITY PRESS
CAMBRIDGE
LONDON · NEW YORK · MELBOURNE

PA
6646
S8

Published by the Syndics of the Cambridge University Press
The Pitt Building, Trumpington Street, Cambridge CB2 1RP
Bentley House, 200 Euston Road, London NW1 2DB
32 East 57th Street, New York, NY 10022, USA
296 Beaconsfield Parade, Middle Park, Melbourne 3206, Australia

First published 1976

Printed in the United States of America
by Vail-Ballou Press, Inc., Binghamton, New York

Library of Congress Cataloguing in Publication Data

Sullivan, John Patrick.

Propertius.

Bibliography: p.
Includes indexes.
1. Propertius, Sextus Aurelius.
PA6646.S8   874'.01 [B]   75-10038
ISBN 0 521 20904 8

Acknowledgments
The extract from *Properce, ou les amants de Tibur* by Julien
Benda is reproduced by permission of Editions Bernard
Grasset, Paris. The extract from *Poets in a Landscape* by
Gilbert Highet, © by Gilbert Highet, published 1957
by Alfred A. Knopf Inc., is reproduced by permission of the
publishers. The extract from the *Oxford Classical Dictionary*, ©
Oxford University Press 1970, is reproduced by permission of the
Oxford University Press, Oxford. Lines from 'Portrait of a
Lady' and 'The Waste Land' in *Collected Poems* 1909–1962 by
T. S. Eliot, © 1936 by Harcourt Brace Jovanovich Inc.; © 1963,
1964 by T. S. Eliot. Reprinted by permission of the
publishers. Lines from 'Homage to Sextus Propertius' in
Personae by Ezra Pound, © 1926 by Ezra Pound. Reprinted by
permission of New Directions Publishing Corporation.

Ecquid, quaeso, nostra interest Antiquitatis studium, si ab iis, quae olim facta sunt, orationem nesciamus ad haec citeriora et notiora nobis deducere?

Vincenzo Padula

CONTENTS

PREFACE

In his preface to his study of Horace's satires in 1966 Niall Rudd complained that there was no comprehensive book in English on Propertius, Persius, Petronius, Lucan, or Pliny. Rudd, of course, was not implying any lack of general or scholarly interest in Propertius. Numerous monographs, articles, and editions have appeared in recent years, but there is still no standard introduction in English to which one may with confidence refer the neophyte classicist or even a non-classical colleague whose primary interest may be Ezra Pound, but who wishes to acquire sufficient knowledge to appreciate the difference between the Propertius we know and the Propertius presented by Pound in his *Homage to Sextus Propertius.**

This remark is not to be taken as a criticism of Pound's interesting poem; indeed, no little credit must be given to him for restoring Propertius in some degree to the public domain by drawing him to the attention of other poets such as Robert Lowell, and arousing a greater interest in his political and literary attitudes. Before then Propertian studies had been mainly concerned with textual criticism and exegesis, apart from a mildly prurient curiosity about the poet's affair with Cynthia. It would be wrong of course to attribute this enlarged investigation of Propertius solely to Ezra Pound, although the scant credit given him by most classical scholars is a disgrace to the profession. On the one hand, our insight into the nature of Augustan politics and literature has been sharpened by our own political experiences in the past several decades, and not least by Sir

---

* Regrettably, Steele Commager, *A Prolegomenon to Propertius* (Cincinnati, 1974) and Margaret Hubbard, *Propertius* (London, 1974) came into my hands too late to take notice of in my text.

Ronald Syme's crystallization of that change in the *Zeitgeist*
with the publication in 1939 of *The Roman Revolution*. On the
other hand, a growing and more sophisticated study of Hellenistic literature and its influence on classical Latin authors has
sharpened our feeling for the complexity of Propertius' literary
theory and practice.

The picture of Propertius the love-poet, whose lyric romanti-
cism is only marred by poor texts and obscure language and
whose only concern is Cynthia except in a handful of ill-
conceived aetiological and panegyrical elegies, is going into the
limbo to which we relegated Vergil the Magician and Ovid the
Preceptor of Courtly Love. In this book I attempt to articulate
the more complex figure that is now assumed in modern Propertian studies.

An introduction such as this should not, of course, try to cover
everything. So I have not dealt with the many problems of the
transmission and emendation of Propertius' text and the extant
MSS; discussion of Propertius' reputation is deliberately cursory
and concentrates principally on the revival of Propertian studies
in the twentieth century; and naturally no attempt has been
made to analyse every poem in the *oeuvre*. Footnotes have been
kept to a minimum. They record generally the source of some
ideas I subscribe to or disagree with; or articles and dissertations that might otherwise escape the student's notice. I should
add that many of the points I make will be familiar and many
of those not so familiar will have much in common with theories
proposed by other Propertian scholars. Since I have been nig-
gardly with notes and my memory is not always trustworthy, I
would like to take a leaf from Wittgenstein's book and state that
'if my remarks do not bear a stamp which shows that they are
mine, I do not wish to lay any further claim to them as my
property'. The standard literature on Propertius may be easily
assembled from the select bibliography I append. One hopes
that Propertius himself approved of Callimachus' dictum: τὸ
μέγα βιβλίον ἴσον τῷ μεγάλῳ κακῷ.

Some of the arguments and views advanced here have appeared elsewhere in different forms, in *Arion, Arethusa, Classical Quarterly, The Kenyon Review, Essays in Criticism, Wiener
Studien, The American Journal of Philology, The Times Literary*

Supplement and in *Ezra Pound and Sextus Propertius: A Study in Creative Translation* (Austin, Texas, 1964), a book which, being directed to those interested in modern poetry, is unlikely to be familiar to classical reviewers or students of Latin literature.

I am grateful for the scholarly advice or criticism of Leo C. Curran, Lawrence Richardson, Jr, Judith P. Hallett, the anonymous reader of the Cambridge University Press and, in particular, William R. Nethercut, who also read the proofs. This book would not have been begun or finished without the encouragement of various editors in the New York office of the Cambridge University Press: Elizabeth Case, Jane Alpert and Sarah Shields. To them and my patient secretaries, Doris Michaels, Barbara Woodruff, Sandra Fazekas, Lorraine Harf and Mary Ann Lewis, my sincere thanks. For the forbearance and help of my wife, Judy Godfrey, words fail me – *ingenium nobis ipsa puella facit!*

State University of New York at Buffalo
August 1974   J.P.S.

ABBREVIATIONS

AJP   *American Journal of Philology*
BICS   *Bulletin of the Institute of Classical Studies*
        of the University of London
CJ   *The Classical Journal*
CP   *Classical Philology*
GRBS   *Greek, Roman and Byzantine Studies*
H   *Hermes*
HSCP   *Harvard Studies in Classical Philology*
JRS   *Journal of Roman Studies*
Latomus
        Latomus, Revue d'études latines
PCPhS *Proceedings of the Cambridge Philological Society*
Pf.   R. Pfeiffer, *Callimachus*: vol. I *Fragmenta*[2]
        (Oxford 1965)
RAL   *Rendiconti della Classe di Scienze Morali, Storiche,*
        Filologiche dell'Accademia dei Lincei, Roma
RE   Pauly–Wissowa, *Real-Encyclopädie der classischen*
        Altertumswissenschaft, Stuttgart 1894
REL   *Revue des Études Latines*
RFIC   *Rivista di Filologia e di Istruzione Classica,*
        Torino
RhM   *Rheinisches Museum für Philologie*
TAPA   *Transactions and Proceedings of the American*
        Philological Society
WS   *Wiener Studien, Zeitschrift für Klassische*
        Philologie (und Patristik)
YCS   *Yale Classical Studies*

MAGISTRIS DISCIPULISQUE
FACULTATIS
ARTIUM ET LITTERARUM
APUD UNIVERSITATEM PUBLICAM
NOVI EBURACI
IN URBE BELLI FLUVII SITAM
SINE QUIBUS HOC OPUSCULUM
IAM DIU PERFECISSEM

1
PROPERTIUS' LIFE AND
LITERARY FORTUNES

Early life

Not far from Etruscan Perugia, the small hill town of Assisi rises above the Umbrian plain. Apart from St Francis, its most prominent son was Sextus Propertius.[1] The general area has a number of inscriptions relating to the Propertii and to the Passenni, who we learn from Pliny the Younger (6.15, 9.22) were connected to the Propertii. These allow us to infer without certainty that Propertius' family belonged to the equestrian class or, at least, to the propertied landowners of the area (4.1.129). Establishing the date of his birth is difficult, but it is important not to let his precocious poetic and amorous talents blind us to the general drift of the evidence. Most authorities put it around 48 B.C., although conservative opinion, forgetting the examples of Lucan, Chatterton and Keats, pushes it back as far as 54 or earlier.

His early years, in any case, were spent in horrendous times of civil war. His father died, perhaps a casualty of war, when he was only a child, which perhaps produced a dependency and a closeness to his mother which would have some effect on his later erotic life. It would at least foster the importance of the maternal image and perhaps lead to his preference for an older woman such as Cynthia. His relatives clearly took the wrong side in the civil war between the followers of Antony and Octavian. The penultimate poem in his first book refers to the death of a close relative following the siege of Perusia, the modern Perugia, when Octavian bloodily and ferociously starved the army of Lucius Antonius into surrender in 41 B.C. However we date his birth, Propertius was old enough to know and re-

1 Cf. 1.22.1–3, 9–10; 4.1.61–6; 4.1.121–6.

member his kinsman. The subsequent reduction of his family estate by the distribution of his (or his father's) lands among the veterans of Octavian and Antony left an additional mark on his memory, which was to show itself in his political attitudes to the principate and in his strong allegiance to his Etruscan connections. We may assume that his mother, whom he was to lose before the publication of his second book, brought him to Rome in his early adolescence, just as Catullus' family had brought him from Verona. There was, after all, little opportunity in the small towns of Italy for a bright and ambitious boy to rise. But as with Catullus and Ovid, Propertius' ambitions did not follow the conventional Roman mould. Legal, political, and military careers, though not incompatible with the practice of elegy, witness Gallus and Tibullus, were not for Propertius (4.1.133–6). Art, sensuality, and romance were for him, as for Ovid, the preferred mode of life: aspirations to fame were to be satisfied by the power of the pen. However unreliable the details, Propertius' life as a young man about town is chronicled in his first book. Unlike Persius, he had no Cornutus to save him from the wrong choice when he got the freedom all well-to-do Roman youths got when they donned the *toga virilis* (at the age of sixteen or earlier) and entered manhood. Unlike Horace, he may have lacked the means to continue his education at Athens (cf. 1.6; 3.21), although his plaint may be simply the elaboration of a conventional theme.

If the less conservative chronology is correct, then Propertius' passionate involvement with Cynthia came at a very early age by modern standards. Romance of course is not a prerogative of youth, but young men think it is, and our myths reinforce this belief. Rome afforded easy access to women of all sorts, and Propertius' first recorded adventure was with Lycinna, the slave of his beloved Cynthia (3.15.6, 43), chosen perhaps because Cynthia was not then available to him.

Cynthia was somewhat older than Propertius. She was probably a high-class *meretrix*, a courtesan, talented as well as sensual, who in return for the proper consideration involved herself on a long- or short-term basis with various lovers, although the possibility cannot be excluded that she was a married woman with a fairly complaisant or easily deceived husband.[2] The relationship was a stormy one and lasted, if we can trust Propertius' poetic evidence, something like five years until their final break. She died not many years afterwards.

Chronology of his poetry

Beyond these probabilities, attempts to reconstruct in detail the actual course of Propertius' affair with Cynthia, because of the conventions of elegy, indeed of poetry in general, must be rejected. Book 1, the so-called *Monobiblos*, probably appeared sometime before 28 B.C., when the poet was twenty or so, and brought him immediate fame, although it is fairly clear from the persons addressed in the first book, Bassus the iambic poet, Ponticus the epic poet, and Tullus, a member of an originally Etruscan family and the nephew of L. Volcacius Tullus, consul in 33 B.C., that Propertius was well established in the social and literary circles to which Ovid would later belong (*Tr.* 4.10.45ff.) and there hear him recite.

The opening of Book 2 is addressed to Maecenas, as is elegy 9 of Book 3. There is no mention of him in Book 4. Could it be that the poet's *succès d'estime* did not endure in the most important circle of all, where Vergil and Horace dominated?

If we go by the latest datable events in the traditional division of Propertius' books, it would seem that Book 2 was published sometime in or after 26 B.C.; Book 3, sometime after 23 B.C.; and Book 4, sometime in or after 16 B.C. We know from Ovid (*Rem.Am.* 764) *that* Propertius was dead by 2 B.C., and Pliny's references to Passennus Paulus, himself an elegist and a self-avowed descendant of the poet, indicate that Propertius finally did his duty: he married and had children. It has also been conjectured, despite the highly artistic arrangement of Book 4, that it was edited and published posthumously.

2 See Gordon Williams, *Tradition and Originality in Roman Poetry* (Oxford 1968) 529ff. Certain elegies in which Propertius has easy access to Cynthia and she to him or where she is waiting for his arrival at her home tell against this theory (cf. e.g. 2.9, 14, 15, 29; 3.8, 16; 4.8).

This traditional chronology, however, has been recently challenged by Gordon Williams.[3] He propounds the theory that the first three books, more or less as we have them in our present texts, were published as a collection like Horace's first three books of *Odes*. As this is a matter of some moment for our view of Propertius' poetic career, it might be well to examine the evidence upon which such a theory is based.

Martial's view of the *Monobiblos* as a pleasing present (*Cynthia − facundi carmen iuvenale Properti*: 14.189) and the fact that Propertius ends the book with a brief epigram (*sphragis*) describing his origins and homeland, would indicate that the book was published separately. The chief evidence Williams adduces for his thesis is the famous passage at 2.13.25 where Propertius pictures himself taking three books as gifts to Persephone after his death.

Williams believes that the book Martial praises was just a convenient selection and since Propertius, in publishing his poems, more or less preserved the chronological order of their composition, this 'youthful production' need not refer to an early attempt to put his work before the public, since private and semi-public circulation was perfectly adequate for this. At 2.3.4 Propertius alludes to 'a second disgraceful book' with little time (*mensem*) intervening after the first about his love life. At 2.13.25 he wants only to take *tres libelli* in his funeral *cortège* to Persephone. This could be a reasonable, if pessimistic, prediction of his output; it could be a satisfactory magic number to invoke; but Williams takes it as evidence that he was proposing to publish his first three books as a 'single unit', describing, among other things, his relationship with Cynthia from the beginning to the end. There is, I believe, an implicit assumption here that Propertius put into the *Monobiblos* all he had written so far. But given the careful symmetry of that book and the balance most Augustan poets liked in their published works, is this likely? Did Horace include *all* the lyric poems he had written in *Odes* 1 − 3? Propertius' selection for Book 1 could easily have been made from a larger mass of available material. There

3 *Tradition and Originality*, 480ff.

is certainly metrical evidence that earlier elegies were incorporated into later books.

The external evidence is admittedly scanty and disputable. When, however, we look at the internal, perhaps more subjective, evidence, it is still hard to accept Williams' basic thesis. He argues that since Cynthia dominates all three books, although references to her become more and more infrequent, then they must have been conceived as a unit.

Williams accepts the fact that there is a distinct movement in Propertius, perhaps through Tibullan influence, towards the disyllabic Ovidian pentameter endings in the four books as we have them (namely: 61%, 86%, 95%, 98%). His explanation is that Propertius more or less preserved the chronological order of his writing. If, on the other hand, one looks at the statistics for individual elegies, it seems as though Books 2 and 3 are fairly consistent in their move towards the disyllabic norm, but Book 1 is somewhat uneven in this, thus destroying Williams' thesis that Propertius kept roughly to the chronological order of writing when he published his poems. For example in Book 1 such elegies as 7, 9, 10, 13, and 19 are much closer to Propertius' later metrical norm. This offers support to O. Skutsch's thesis that certain later poems were introduced into Book 1 to provide it with the necessary symmetry and ballast.[4] Books 2 and 3 (as we have them) are much more consistent, although certain traces of earlier work, perhaps now polished, survive in them, as is indicated by the higher number of polysyllabic pentameter endings in certain elegies (e.g. 2.20, 31, 34). Therefore stylistic analysis indicates that the chronology of Propertius' poetry can hardly be a linear one. Though we may be justified on the basis of the scant historical references in saying that such-and-such a book *cannot* have been published before a certain date, we must not assume that all the material in a given

4 O. Skutsch, 'The structure of the Propertian *Monobiblos*', *CP* 58 (1963) 238–9. Skutsch argues convincingly for a symmetrical arrangement of the poems in Book 1, necessitating even a deliberate creation of poems to secure this symmetry. Whatever the disagreements about the details, there is in Book 1, with its author's seal in the last short elegy, a very self-conscious structure, which critics have tried in vain to find in Book 2.

book was written after the completion (or publication) of its predecessor. Some other relevant facts may be adduced. Book 1 has twenty (or twenty-one) elegies followed by two short epigrams. Book 3 has twenty-five elegies. Book 4 has twelve elegies. The lines number 686, 990 and 952 respectively. Book 2 alone has 43 elegies and 1,328 lines. If the poets of the Augustan Age were as careful about construction, symmetry, and variation as we know they were, it is unlikely that Book 2 could have been issued from the hands of its author as it was. Whatever the accidents of transmission, tradition, or misfortune that have produced the present state of Book 2, it seems clear that this is where the explanation for these troublesome lines of Propertius on his gift to Persephone is to be found. The range of themes in Books 2 and 3 is far greater than in Book 1. This might be discounted on grounds of chronological development, but the great divergency of addressees cannot be so easily shrugged off. If we exclude Cynthia we find that in Book 1 Gallus is addressed four times, Tullus three, Ponticus twice, and Bassus once. Ponticus is not addressed again, unless he is the Demophoon of 2.22 and Tullus is addressed again only in 3.22. In fact, named addressees, except for two important elegies addressed to Maecenas, are very uncommon in the last three books. Were the first three books put together and published as a unit, one would have expected some greater consistency in this complimentary practice. Williams compares their publication to that of Horace's *Odes* 1–3, but the careful arrangement of each of Horace's books, their comparable length (e.g. Odes 1 and 3 are approximately the same size[5]), their consistent admixture of themes and addressees make this a very inappropriate analogy, and Ovid's second edition of the *Amores* in three books indicates what a careful arrangement one might also expect from an elegist.

Book 4, which introduces a totally new note in Propertius' works, was published either by the poet or posthumously. In any case, its arrangement does credit to the author or the editor

5 Book 2 of the *Odes* was clearly meant to be a centre for the other two books, see W. Ludwig, 'Zu Horaz, C. 2.1–12', *H* 85 (1957) 336–45.

and it should be regarded as a separate phase of the poet's career.

It is best therefore to postulate an early, middle, and late stage in Propertius' poetic development. A separate publication for each of Books 1 and 4 is indicated. But although we cannot entirely exclude separate publication of Books 2 and 3, somewhat in the form we now have them, the various datable allusions and the pronounced differences between them with regard to pentameter endings make more plausible K. Lachmann's theory, which was also based on 2.13.25 *(tres libelli)*.[6] Lachmann postulated an edition of three books, which in the course of time was considerably mutilated in various ways. This might explain the bloatedness and unevenness of Book 2, which, in the words of one critic, L. J. Richardson, presents us now with a text reminiscent of a 'mass of spaghetti'. In its present shape, it would certainly have been no fit companion for that elegant gift Martial so praised.

The three stages in Propertius' career, I would suggest, are represented by the initial and momentous Book 1, the three Books that presently comprise our Books 2 and 3 and then, somewhat later, the radically changed style and content of Book 4.

There is no room here to discuss where the division of Book 2 should be made. There are various theories, just as there have been various futile attempts to descry an ordered structure in this book. The possibility of severe textual disruptions in the elegies as they stand makes a decision harder to reach. Indeed, the game is profitless if one takes the view, fortified by the confusion of statistics in the individual elegies, that we are dealing with a re-edited set of poems which might have been perfectly clear sequentially in their original ordered form.

If the above account is correct, then the chronology of Propertius' poetry must become somewhat more tentative. We may assume that Book 1 was published before October 28 B.C., since elegy 31 in Book 2 celebrates the inauguration of Apollo's temple on that date. Nevertheless, although in Book 2, elegy 34 refers to the death of Cornelius Gallus in 26 B.C., we no

6 See the introduction to *Sexti Aurelii Propertii Carmina* (Leipzig 1816) pp. xixff.

longer have to assume that the *whole* of our present Book 2 was published after this date. We may now entertain the idea that the original Book 2 could have been published between 28 and 26 or else, following to this extent Williams' theory, the whole collection of the three books of elegies which now comprise our present Books 2 and 3 were published together sometime before the settlement with the Parthians in 20 B.C. There would, of course, be no need after the publication of the first book for an elegist to produce the regular thin volume at two- or three-yearly intervals that we require from our budding younger poets. There were many opportunities for informal and oral publication: semi-public recitations, the circulation of manuscripts among friends, particularly among those connected with Maecenas' circle, and so on. The long gestation of Vergil's *Aeneid* did not lessen his fame once the *Eclogues* were published around 37 B.C. This would have been enough to prompt the salutations of the crowd in the theatre referred to by Tacitus (*Dial.* 13). Book 4 of course cannot have been published before 16 B.C., as a reference in the Cornelia elegy (4.11) to her brother's consulship in that year makes obvious.

Literary life in Rome

Whatever the age Propertius was when he took up residence in Rome, it is clear that, like Ovid, he took up the craft of poetry early, stimulated no doubt by the inordinate literary activity of the period. We do well to remind ourselves of the enduring masterpieces that emerged during Propertius' lifetime and to whose composition he was privy, not to mention the records we have of poets such as Varius Rufus and Valgius, whose works have almost entirely vanished.[7] Around 37 B.C. Vergil had published his *Eclogues*. In 35 B.C., Horace's first book of satires had appeared; around 30, the second book and the *Epodes*; late in 23, his collection of *Odes* were published in three books. 30 B.C. is a not unlikely date for the publication of Vergil's *Georgics*. Tibullus was active during this crucial period and Gallus was widely read before his suicide in 26 B.C.

7 See H. Bardon, *La Littérature latine inconnue* II (Paris 1956) 11–77.

What part the literary circles of the time played in Propertius' development as a poet is a subject of some speculation. If we accept the traditional view, contested by Williams, that the *Monobiblos* gave Propertius some sort of entrée to the circle of Maecenas, signalized by the initial programmatic elegy of Book 2, we must also realize that, even by the time he published the first book, he had literary and social acquaintances worth addressing in individual poems (notably, Bassus, Ponticus, and Tullus). In his first book, Propertius was most influenced by Catullus and Gallus, but the influence, and the mediated Alexandrianism, is limited, showing itself most clearly in the variation on the *paraclausithyron*[8] (1.16) and the *epyllion* on the rape of Hylas (1.20). What is most noticeable in the book is the autobiographical stress on his relationship with Cynthia, a specifically Roman note that he owed to Catullus, just as in satire and epistolography it had been well established by Lucilius and Cicero.

Admission to wider circles of acquaintance and to further familiarity with the literary theories discussed and artistically embodied would perhaps explain the greater self-consciousness about his art that Propertius reveals in Book 2 and after. Although the aesthetic implications of all this will be discussed in a later chapter, one may glance briefly at the historical circumstances of patronage and literary production that Propertius must have encountered and, as I shall argue, found unfavourable or distasteful.

Systematic patronage was a prominent feature of the time. The Scholiast on Horace reports that Vergil and Varius each received one million sesterces from the emperor and, according to Suetonius' *Life of Vergil*, that poet's earnings were ten million. No doubt these figures are exaggerated, but Horace's own works indicate that the poets of his circle did indeed receive munificent gifts. Nor, to judge from Horace's poems to Maecenas, was the reward purely financial. Friendship with the

8 The theme is first seen in literature with Alcaeus (374), occurs frequently in comedy and was very popular with the writers of the Greek Anthology. Catullus' dialogue with a door may have prompted Propertius to write this soliloquy *from* the door. Even Horace utilized the basic theme (*Od.* 1.25; 3.10.19–20).

great, in a society which depended so much upon personal alliances and political protection, was in itself no small reward, particularly when one considers the misfortunes of certain earlier republican writers who had had no such protection. Two patrons stand out above all others: Messala and Maecenas; both of them were scholarly or literary men. With Messala are associated Tibullus and Ovid, as well as a number of lesser poets. Maecenas' great catches were, of course, Vergil, Varius, and Horace, but there were many others: Tucca, Domitius Marsus, C. Melissus, to name but a few. By the time of Martial, Maecenas had become the paradigm of the patron. We need not view such a literary circle as this in terms of crass monetary dependence, although that was clearly available as a lever in the case of the poorer writers of the period. It is rather that in such a caste-ridden society as Rome, *dignitas* was attached to both *gloria* and *auctoritas*. The complaints of Horace about his poverty, certainly those of Tibullus, and perhaps those of Propertius, are part of a poetic convention and are probably exaggerated. But, whatever the leverage used, there can be no doubt, as Syme has suggested,[9] that Octavian, through Maecenas, was interested in forming a favourable climate of opinion about his now autocratic rule. Pressures of all sorts could be applied, however subtly. To be the acquaintance of a man whom so many poets regarded as a friend would in itself be an attraction to the highly emulatory poets of the period. The later works of Ovid reveal how interested poets of the period were in the works of their contemporaries and in claiming their friendship. To be 'in' was apparently as important in Rome as it now is in New York or London. But since, whatever the human or baser motives that existed on both sides, the poets of the age were indeed literary theorists and craftsmen of a high order, we may also surmise that the discussions of literary principles were as important as simply hobnobbing with the great and famous. As with all coteries, there would also be rivalries and it is at this point that one has to examine the ambiguous attitude of Propertius to Maecenas.

That some sort of rivalry emerged between Horace and Pro-

9 *The Roman Revolution* 251ff.; 459ff.

pertius is likely; but that Horace was closer to Maecenas than
Propertius is certain. And one possible reason for Horace's dislike of Propertius is to be found in the odes addressed to Tibullus
(if the plausible identification is accepted). As we shall see
later, the aims of the now central poets of the Augustan tradition, Vergil and Horace, were alien to the literary practice and
principles of the elegists. Tibullus, belonging to the circle of
Messala, can be implored to abandon his *flebiles elegos* with
good humour. Propertius' pretensions, to judge from Horace's
allusions to them, and his determined attitudes were perhaps not
so easily brushed aside. Besides, Tibullus, despite his elegist's
pose, had seen some military service. Propertius' attitude to
this, as is clear from certain poems, was completely contemptuous, except when he was pretending interest before turning
away from the grand themes of empire. Both Horace and Vergil
had their detractors, as we know in particular from Horace's
letter to Augustus (*Ep.* 2.1), and Horace took on his 'classically
minded' critics with gusto, but that in no way implied that he
did not have similar critical feelings about other practitioners of
the poetic art who were his contemporaries. A slighting remark
in Horace about Catullus and Calvus would indicate that he
felt particular hostility to the self-proclaimed 'true' Alexandrians
of the Roman period, not least Propertius (*Sat.* 1.10).

Propertius' relationship then with Maecenas' circle was not
particularly close, even though these circles were not tight,
unified coteries, but had considerable overlapping with other
friends and groups. As it happens, both of the poems in which
Maecenas is addressed (2.1; 3.9) are paradigmatic examples of
the *recusatio*,[10] the refusal to write, for one reason or another,
on themes which the poet finds himself unequal to, or disin-
clined for. It is not difficult to conclude therefore that his literary and political principles may have been reinforced in this
context by some personal or ideological uneasiness in the literary
life of Rome.

It is clear however that he was familiar with work in progress
such as the *Aeneid* (2.34.66); that he gave recitations (Ov. *Tr.*
4.10.45–6); and that he was no recluse. Nor was he retiring

10 See below, pp. 122–7

in his claims to fame, if we can take at face value Horace's sneer at the 'Roman Callimachus' (*Ep.* 2.2.91ff.).

Propertius, Horace and Vergil

The literary relationship between Horace and Propertius may throw some light on the place of Propertius in the larger literary scene and so it merits closer scrutiny. Allusions to Horace's first three books of *Odes* have been frequently remarked upon by commentators,[11] but not enough has been made of these allusions. The proud tone of the opening lines of 3.1,

> Callimachi manes et Coi sacra Philitae
> in vestrum, quaeso, me sinite ire nemus.
> primus ego ingredior puro de fonte sacerdos
> Itala per Graios orgia ferre choros.

Shades of Callimachus and rites of Coan Philitas, admit me to your grove, I beg. First am I to enter, a priest from an unsullied fount, to bear sacred symbols of Italy amid Greek worshippers

is meant as a direct challenge to the Roman Alcaeus, who had claimed to be:

> ex humili potens
> princeps Aeolium carmen ad Italos
> deduxisse modos.   (*Od.* 3.30.12–14)

mighty from small beginnings, leader in adapting Aeolian song to Italian rhythms.

Book 3 is Propertius' counter to Horace's *Odes*. There he expresses firmly his adherence to love, peace, and amatory elegy

---

11 See e.g. F. Solmsen, 'Propertius and Horace', *CP* 43 (1948) 105–9; D. Flach, *Das literarische Verhältnis von Horaz und Properz* (Giessen 1967). The clearest statement of the case that Propertius' allusions to Horace are complimentary is N. Terzaghi, 'Orazio e Properzio', *Studia Graeca et Latina* (Turin 1963) 1174–96.

that Horace, as we know from his odes to Albius (1.33) and Valgius, professed to despise:

> desine mollium
> tandem querelarum, et potius nova
> cantemus Augusti tropaea
> Caesaris   (*Od.* 2.9.17ff.)

cease finally your unmanly plaints and rather let us celebrate the new trophies of Augustus Caesar.

A direct response to that is of course a part of the first programmatic elegy of Book 3:

> a valeat, Phoebum quicumque moratur in armis!
>   exactus tenui pumice versus eat, —
> quo me Fama levat terra sublimis, et a me
>   nata coronatis Musa triumphat equis,
> et mecum in curru parvi vectantur Amores,
>   scriptorumque meas turba secuta rotas.
> quid frustra missis in me certatis habenis?
>   non datur ad Musas currere lata via.
> multi, Roma, tuas laudes annalibus addent,
>   qui finem imperii Bactra futura canent.
> sed, quod pace legas, opus hoc de monte Sororum
>   detulit intacta pagina nostra via.
> mollia, Pegasides, date vestro serta poetae:
>   non faciet capiti dura corona meo.   (7–20)

The tone of this is well caught by Ezra Pound's poetic paraphrase:

> Out-weariers of Apollo will, as we know, continue their
>   Martian generalities,
>   We have kept our erasers in order.
> A new-fangled chariot follows the flower-hung horses;
> A young Muse with young loves clustered about her
>   ascends with me into the aether, . . .
> And there is no high-road to the Muses.
> Annalists will continue to record Roman reputations,

> Celebrities from the Trans-Caucasus will belaud Roman
>   celebrities
> And expound the distentions of Empire,
> But for something to read in normal circumstances?
> For a few pages brought down from the forked hill
>   unsullied?
> I ask a wreath which will not crush my head.

Pound clearly understood the significance of this poem since he chose to make it the opening translation of *Homage to Sextus Propertius*. If we look at the structure of Book 3 we find that, as with *Odes* 3, Propertius puts forward his literary and social theory first, in five defiant elegies. He defends his own stance in contrast to the stance of the poet who wrote the six great Augustan odes. He stresses the lover's devotion to peace (3.5); his own rejection of warlike themes (3.1.15–16) whether derived from the glory of Rome's past (3.3.3–12) or contemporary imperialist ventures (3.4); and, with little indirectness, his contempt for those who wish to recover the lost standards of Crassus from the Parthians (3.5.47–8).

The ninth elegy of this book, indeed, is not only a refusal to handle such grand themes but also a careful, glancing reply to Horace's *Odes* 1.1. In a subtle and ironic tone, characteristic of the writers of *lusus* and *nugae*, Propertius seems to be saying to Horace and all concerned that he, Propertius, is the great elegist of love and he therefore follows the pattern of Horace's dedicatory address to Maecenas very specifically. In that prefatory ode Horace made his claim to be classed with Alcaeus and Pindar:

> Maecenas atavis edite regibus, . . .
> quodsi me lyricis vatibus inseres
> sublimi feriam sidera vertice (*Od.* 1.1.1, 35–6)

> *Maecenas, born of ancient kings . . . if you will put me*
> *among the lyric bards, I will strike the stars with my*
> *head.*

Propertius, like Horace, takes us through the different pursuits and talents of men, but by a clever twist he is able to connect this old theme to Maecenas himself. Few commentators have realized the significance of this.

> Maecenas, eques Etrusco de sanguine regum,
>   intra fortunam qui cupis esse tuam,
> quid me scribendi tam vastum mittis in aequor?
>   non sunt apta meae grandia vela rati . . .
> at tua, Maecenas, vitae praecepta recepi,
>   cogor et exemplis te superare tuis.
> cum tibi Romano dominas in honore secures
>   et liceat medio ponere iura foro,
> vel tibi Medorum pugnaces ire per hastas,
>   atque onerare tuam fixa per arma domum;
> et tibi ad effectum vires det Caesar, et omni
>   tempore tam faciles insinuentur opes,
> parcis et in tenues humilem te colligis umbras:
>   velorum plenos subtrahis ipse sinus.
> crede mihi, magnos aequabunt ista Camillos
>   iudicia, et venies tu quoque in ora virum,
> Caesaris et famae vestigia iuncta tenebis:
>   Maecenatis erunt vera tropaea fides.
> non ego velifera tumidum mare findo carina:
>   tuta sub exiguo flumine nostra mora est.
> non flebo in cineres arcem sedisse paternos
>   Cadmi, nec septem proelia clade pari,
> nec referam Scaeas et Pergama, Apollinis arces,
>   et Danaum decimo vere redisse rates,
> moenia cum Graio Neptunia pressit aratro
>   victor Palladiae ligneus artis equus.
> inter Callimachi sat erit placuisse libellos
>   et cecinisse modis, Coe poeta, tuis.
> haec urant pueros, haec urant scripta puellas,
>   meque deum clament et mihi sacra ferant!
> te duce vel Iovis arma canam caeloque minantem
>   Coeum et Phlegraeis Eurymedonta iugis,
> celsaque Romanis decerpta Palatia tauris
>   ordiar et caeso moenia firma Remo
> eductosque pares silvestri ex ubere reges,
>   crescet et ingenium sub tua iussa meum;

prosequar et currus utroque ab litore ovantes,
   Parthorum astutae tela remissa fugae,
castraque Pelusi Romano subruta ferro
   Antonique graves in sua fata manus.
mollis tu coeptae fautor cape lora iuventae
   dexteraque inmissis da mihi signa rotis!
hoc mihi, Maecenas, laudis concedis, et a te est,
   quod ferar in partes ipse fuisse tuas. (1–4, 21ff.)

*Maecenas, knight of kingly Etruscan blood, you who
wish to stay within your station, why do you launch
me on so vast an ocean of writing? Great sails are not
suitable for my craft . . . No, Maecenas, I have taken
your precepts about life to heart and I must defeat you
by your own example. When you could plant the imperial axes as a Roman magistrate and deal out justice
in the heart of the Forum or ride through the warlike
spears of the Medes and fill up your house with captured weapons and when Caesar would give you powers
for the purpose and when at any time such easy re-
sources would come flowing in, you hold back and you
withdraw humbly into the background like a man of no
importance: you yourself reef in the full billows of your
sails. Believe me, these decisions will equal those of
the great heroes such as Camillus, and you also will live
on men's lips. You will stand linked to Caesar's fame:
loyalty will be the real trophies of Maecenas. It is not
for me to cleave the swelling sea with sail-laden ship:
I shall not tearfully relate the fall of the citadel of Cad-
mus over the ashes of the fathers and seven battles ending in equal disaster; I shall not tell of the Scaean gates
and Apollo's citadel of Pergamum and the return of the
Greek ships in the tenth spring, when the wooden horse,
built by the art of Pallas, victoriously demolished Nep-
tune's walls with the Greek plough. It will be enough
for me to have given pleasure along with Callimachus'
little volumes and to have written poetry in the style of
Philitas. Let these writings fire both boys and girls, and
let them acclaim me divine and worship me.*

> *If you lead the way,* then *I will sing even of the arms of Jupiter and Coeus threatening heaven and Euryme-don on the Phlegraean heights and of the high Palatine grazed by Roman bulls and I will tell of the walls strengthened by Remus' death and of the twin kings reared by an udder in the forest. My genius would grow from the pressure of your commands. I will fol-low on with the chariots triumphing over both shores, the bows unstrung through the astute retreat of the Parthians, the Pelusian camp overthrown by Roman steel and the blow from his own hands that killed Antony. An indulgent supporter of my youthful attempts, take the reins and give me favourable signals for my speed-ing chariot. This honour you grant me, Maecenas, and it is through you that even I myself will be said to belong to your side.*

This is, of course, a much more complex poem than Horace's deferential ode. Propertius, with apparent playfulness, insists that, although he is not capable of writing epic and each must follow his own bent, he offers to write epic if Maecenas will do so first. Behind the courteous bow to Maecenas in this poem, there is also a very palpable hit at Horace's dedicatory address to his patron in *Odes* 1.1. This is Propertius' most devastating undercutting of the Augustan literary establishment and his most daring, if somewhat humorous, expression of opposition – and at Maecenas' expense. It satirizes Horace's dedication of his *Odes* by a far subtler poem. Propertius defends his chosen art form by suggesting that he, like Maecenas, has chosen to stay within his limits. In refusing Maecenas' invitation to launch him on the vast sea of epic, Propertius takes the opportunity to chide Horace for his overpraise of Maecenas. Propertius points out that Maecenas is an *eques*, for all his descent from Etruscan kings, who is content with his station, which is not the station of critic to which Horace had exalted him.

   Another hit at Horace is more amusing. Horace's famous ode to Fuscus begins:

> Integer vitae scelerisque purus
> non eget Mauris iaculis neque arcu

> nec venenatis gravida sagittis,
>> Fusce, pharetra,
> sive per Syrtis iter aestuosas
> sive facturus per inhospitalem
> Caucasum vel quae loca fabulosus
>> lambit Hydaspes. (*Od.* 1.22.1ff.)

> *A man of integrity, untainted by crime, does not need Moorish spears, a bow, and a quiver full of poison arrows, Fuscus, whether he is going to travel through the stormy Syrtes or the unfriendly Caucasus or the regions lapped by the fabled Hydaspes.*

Propertius in turn insists that it is the lover who deserves divine protection, not the upright man:

> nec tamen est quisquam, sacros qui laedat amantes:
>> Scironis media sic licet ire via.
> quisquis amator erit, Scythicis licet ambulet oris,
>> nemo adeo ut noceat barbarus esse volet.   (3.16.11ff.)

> *But there is no one who attacks lovers; they are sacred; so they can walk openly on the murderous Sciron's highway. Whoever is a lover, though he may stroll along Scythian shores, no one will be so barbarous as to harm him.*

The most audacious challenge and clearest allusion to Horace is also contained in 3.1. At the end of his three books of *Odes*, Horace had proclaimed:

> Exegi monumentum aere perennius
> regalique situ pyramidum altius,
> quod non imber edax, non Aquilo impotens
> possit diruere aut innumerabilis
> annorum series et fuga temporum.
> non omnis moriar, multaque pars mei
> vitabit Libitinam: usque ego postera
> crescam laude recens, dum Capitolium
> scandet cum tacita virgine pontifex.
> dicar, qua violens obstrepit Aufidus
> et qua pauper aquae Daunus agrestium

regnavit populorum, ex humili potens
princeps Aeolium carmen ad Italos
deduxisse modos. (*Od.* 3.30.1–14)

*I have built a monument more lasting than bronze and
higher than the regal grave of the Pyramids. This no
devouring rain, no uncontrolled North wind can destroy
nor the uncountable procession of the years and the
flight of time. I shall not perish entirely and a large part
of me will elude Death: I shall grow anew in the praise
of posterity, as long as the Pontifex ascends the Capitol
with the silent vestal. I shall be spoken of where the
violent Aufidus rages and where Daunus, poor in water,
has reigned over his rustic peoples, yes, I, mighty from
small beginnings, leader in adapting Aeolian song to
Italian rhythms.*

We have already seen how Propertius contrasted his claim to be
a Roman innovator, but in the Alexandrian tradition, to Horace's
claim here to be the transplanter of the Greek lyric tradition to
Rome, and we have also seen how he rejected Horace's im-
perialistic poetry for work that can be read in peacetime, but
his critique goes deeper. In the same elegy, he takes Horace's
poetic motifs, the symbols for the resistance of death and the
effects of time and treats them in a different but deliberately
allusive way, the echoes being scattered throughout the long
elegy (which is divided, wrongly, into two in the MSS and
most editions):

nam quis equo pulsas abiegno nosceret arces,
    fluminaque Haemonio comminus isse viro,
Idaeum Simoenta Iovis cum prole Scamandro,
    Hectora per campos ter maculasse rotas?
Deiphobumque Helenumque et Pulydamanta et in armis
    qualemcumque Parim vix sua nosset humus.
exiguo sermone fores nunc, Ilion, et tu
    Troia bis Oetaei numine capta dei.
nec non ille tui casus memorator Homerus
    posteritate suum crescere sensit opus.
meque inter seros laudabit Roma nepotes:
    illum post cineres auguror ipse diem . . .

fortunata, meo si qua es celebrata libello!
    carmina erunt formae tot monumenta tuae.
nam neque Pyramidum sumptus ad sidera ducti,
    nec Iovis Elei caelum imitata domus,
nec Mausolei dives fortuna sepulcri
    mortis ab extrema condicione vacant.
aut illis flamma aut imber subducet honores,
    annorum aut tacito pondere victa ruent.
at non ingenio quaesitum nomen ab aevo
    excidet: ingenio stat sine morte decus.

(3.1.25ff; 3.2.17ff.)

*For who would have known of the citadel battered by
the firwood horse and the rivers that fought with Hae-
monian Achilles, Idaean Simois and Scamander, child
of Jupiter, and how the chariot wheels three times
befouled Hector, dragging him through the plains?
Deiphobus, Helenus, Polydamas, and Paris, that sorry
soldier, their own soil would scarcely know them. You
would today be little talked of, Ilium, and you, Troy,
twice captured by the Oetean god [Hercules]. And
Homer, the historian of your fate, has felt his work grow
among posterity. Me also will Rome praise in later generations: I myself prophesy that day after I am ashes . . .
Fortunate is any girl celebrated in my volume! My
poems will be that many memorials of your beauty. For
neither expensive pyramids reared to the stars nor the
temple of Jupiter at Olympia that rivals the heavens
nor the rich wealth of the tomb of Mausolus are free
from the ultimate condition of death. Either fire or rain
will pull down their glories or they will topple, beaten
down by the silent weight of the years. But a name
gained by genius will not be forgotten through time: the
glory genius gains is deathless.*

The whole long elegy really glances at several of Horace's
themes, odes, and subject matters, but the way in which he
challenges Horace's claim to immortality in favour of his erotic
subject and himself, while stressing, as Horace did not, the mor-
tality of pyramids, is typical of Propertius' method.

Sometimes this rivalry had a possibly adverse effect on Propertius' art. I believe that it may be responsible for that much
debated and troublesome elegy 3.11.[12] If it is agreed that Book
3 is Propertius' response to Horace's *Odes*, then it is not surprising that Propertius would feel obliged to take up the theme of
Cleopatra, described so movingly by Horace *(non humilis
mulier)* in the penultimate ode of Book 1. But note the strange
structure of 3.11. Propertius begins by asking why should anyone blame him for being in thrall to a woman:

> Quid mirare, meam si versat femina vitam
>   et trahit addictum sub sua iura virum,
> criminaque ignavi capitis mihi turpia fingis,
>   quod nequeam fracto rumpere vincla iugo?

> *Why are you surprised that a woman rules my life and
> drags me, a man, into bondage, and why do you trump
> up dirty charges about my weakness, because I cannot
> sever the yoke and break the chains?*

He continues briefly with the familiar mythological and historical
allusions illustrating his plight. (One notes, as usual, the paucity
of stories in a patriarchal mythology that are really relevant to
the elegists' situation, Omphale and Hercules being the only
satisfactory *exemplum* in the series.)[13] He then directs most of
the poem against that *femme fatale* of contemporary Roman
history, Cleopatra.

> quid, modo quae nostris opprobria vexerit armis,
>   et famulos inter femina trita suos?
> coniugii obsceni pretium Romana poposcit
>   moenia et addictos in sua regna Patres.
> noxia Alexandria, dolis aptissima tellus,
>   et totiens nostro Memphi cruenta malo,

12 The best discussions of this elegy are E. Paratore, *L'Elegia III,* 11
e gli Atteggiamenti politici di Properzio (Palermo 1936) and
W.R. Nethercut, 'Propertius, 3.11', *TAPA* 102 (1971) 411–43. A
standard interpretation of the poem as 'patriotic' may be found in
W.A. Camps' commentary on Book 3 (Cambridge 1966) 104ff.
13 For the unsatisfactory and vague reference to Jupiter as a possible
illustration of Propertius' domination by Cynthia (*Iuppiter infamat
seque suamque domum,* line 28), see Philip Slater, *The Glory of
Hera* (Boston 1968, 1971), ch. 3 'Sexual Dominance: Zeus', 125ff.

tres ubi Pompeio detraxit harena triumphos!
  tollet nulla dies hanc tibi, Roma, notam.
issent Phlegraeo melius tibi funera campo,
  vel tua si socero colla daturus eras.
scilicet incesti meretrix regina Canopi,
  una Philippeo sanguine adusta nota,
ausa Iovi nostro latrantem opponere Anubim,
  et Tiberim Nili cogere ferre minas,
Romanamque tubam crepitanti pellere sistro,
  baridos et contis rostra Liburna sequi,
foedaque Tarpeio conopia tendere saxo,
  iura dare et statuas inter et arma Mari!
quid nunc Tarquinii fractas iuvat esse secures,
  nomine quem simili vita superba notat,
si mulier patienda fuit? cane, Roma, triumphum
  et longum Augusto salva precare diem!
fugisti tamen in timidi vaga flumina Nili:
  accepere tuae Romula vincla manus.
bracchia spectavi sacris admorsa colubris,
  et trahere occultum membra soporis iter.   (29–54)

*What about the woman who lately brought disgrace to
our warriors, a woman banged even by her own ser-
vants. The price she asked for that filthy union was the
walls of Rome with our senators in bondage and subjection. Wicked Alexandria, land most suited for dirty
tricks, and you, Memphis, so often reddened with blood
to our cost, where the sand stripped Pompey of his
three triumphs! Never will this stigma on Rome be removed. Pompey's death would have been better on the
Phlegraean Fields, even if he were to bow his neck to
his son-in-law. So, the whorish queen of incestuous
Canopus, the only stigma branded on Rome by the
blood of Philip [of Macedon], dared to confront our
Roman Jupiter with barking Anubis; force the Tiber to
endure the threats of the Nile; rout the Roman trumpet
with clacking rattle; pursue Liburnian prows with barge
oars; hang dirty mosquito-nets on the Tarpeian rock,
and hand down verdicts amid the statues and trophies*

*of Marius! What good now is it to have broken the
authority of Tarquin the Proud, branded by a life as
arrogant as his name, if a woman has to be endured!
Rome, sing out 'triumph!' and pray for long years for
Augustus, now you are safe. But the queen fled to the
wandering rivers of frightened Nile: her hands accepted
the chains of Romulus. I saw her arms bitten by the
sacred snakes and her limbs absorbing the hidden and
numbing poison as it travelled.*

The difficulty with the poem is that Propertius moves very
briskly from his opening theme of female domination of the
male into an attack on Cleopatra without showing any sympathy
for, or even directly mentioning, Antony. If we look at the poem
in the context of the previous poems in Book 3, then it is hard
to interpret it as a seriously intended eulogy of Augustus, even
though a few fulsome compliments, as in 3.9, are inserted. There
are too many veiled references to civil war, to Rome's shame,
and to the Roman kings (e.g. lines 35ff., 47f.) for that reading
to be convincing. It has been argued that Propertius, a crypto-
republican rather than an avowed monarchist, would be against
any supreme sovereign, particularly a foreigner and a woman,
but that is scarcely a sufficient explanation for the whole anti-
Cleopatran thrust of the poem, particularly since in his personal
life he is at least ambivalent about Cynthia's sway over himself
and since, in his elegist's posture, he is hardly political in the
way Horace and Vergil are.

The answer to the imbalance, then, must lie in the suggested
relationship of Book 3 to *Odes* 1 – 3. And this suggestion is
reinforced by the deliberate echoes of Horace: compare, for
example, the shared motifs of the Liburnian galleys (3.11.44
and 1.37.30); the snakebites (3.11.53 and 1.37.26f.); the chains
(never in fact used) (3.11.52 and 1.37.20); the flight to Egypt
(3.11.51 and 1.37.24); her disgraceful entourage (3.11.30 and
1.37.9f.); her plans for the Capitol (3.11.45f. and 1.37.6ff.);
the references to the triumph over her (3.11.49, 53 – 5 and
1.37.31f.). As though this were not enough, Propertius uses the
rare word (in poetry) for 'mosquito nets' *(conopium)*. Where
else does this occur? In Juvenal and in Horace's other poem on

Cleopatra, *Epode* 9, which has, of course, a great deal in common with *Odes* 1.37.

It would seem, then, that Propertius, despite the consequences for his poem or for the reader, who would have expected a more logical development of the theme of male subjection, chose to compete directly and unmistakably with Horace's two treatments of the Cleopatra theme. Making the most of his opportunity, he was able both to flatter Augustus as Horace did and also take a sterner line with the *fatale monstrum* than Horace, despite the inconsistency it involved for an elegist who is not too ashamed of being ruled by a woman himself.

These several obvious and tendentious allusions to Horace make more interesting and more ambiguous the well known references to Horace's friend and ally, Vergil, in the triumphant closing elegy of Book 2. It has traditionally been assumed that lines 61–6 are highly complimentary:

> Actia Vergilium [*sc.* iuvet] custodis litora Phoebi,
>   Caesaris et fortes dicere posse rates,
> qui nunc Aeneae Troiani suscitat arma
>   iactaque Lavinis moenia litoribus.
> cedite Romani scriptores, cedite Grai!
>   nescio quid maius nascitur Iliade.

These sentiments Ezra Pound freely but penetratingly translated as:

> Upon the Actian marshes Virgil is Phoebus' chief of
>   police,
>   He can tabulate Caesar's great ships.
> He thrills to Ilian arms,
>   He shakes the Trojan weapons of Aeneas,
>   And casts stores on Lavinian beaches.
> Make way, ye Roman authors,
>   clear the street, O ye Greeks,
> For a much larger Iliad is in the course of construction
>   (and to imperial order)
> Clear the streets, O ye Greeks!

The context of these lines is rarely considered. Propertius is urging his love-lorn friend Lynceus to abandon philosophy and natural science, to turn his back on epic and tragedy, in favour of the work of Philitas and Callimachus, Propertius' own Greek models. Vergil is invoked because of his earlier, more Alexandrian, poetry, the amorous *Eclogues* and the *Georgics* in which any lover may find comfort; Propertius refers to these in complimentary tones, before finally listing the Roman amatory poets, Varro of Atax, Catullus, Calvus, and Gallus, to whose company he hopes Fame will elect him. The bows to the *Aeneid* may thus be seen as purely perfunctory and indeed may be construed as another critical thrust at the Augustan poetical establishment. Propertius, in this poem, makes his preference among Vergil's works quite apparent.

If this interpretation of the literary evidence is correct, then some light is thrown on that much quoted passage in Horace's literary epistle to Florus (2.2), which may be dated to 19 B.C. or later, a few years after the presumed publication of Propertius' third book. Horace complains of his waning talent and inclination for poetry (52–7); he hints at a strong disagreement about the appropriate forms of poetry, when he talks of being unable to please everybody by one type of poetry (58–64). He here mentions lyric, iambic verse and satire as appealing to very different tastes: he is significantly silent about two of the best known Augustan genres: epic and elegy. His sharpest barbs, however, are reserved for the mutual flattery to be found in contemporary poetic circles. It should be remembered that the original edition of Ovid's *Amores*, with their many echoes of Tibullus and Propertius, probably appeared in 20 B.C., when the poet was twenty-three years old. When we compare the reception of the *Odes* with the encouragement clearly given the elegiac poets, Horace's jibes seem to smack of sour grapes.

> frater erat Romae consulti rhetor, ut alter
> alterius sermone meros audiret honores,
> Gracchus ut hic illi, foret huic ut Mucius ille.
> qui minus argutos vexat furor iste poetas?
> carmina compono, hic elegos. 'mirabile visu
> caelatumque novem Musis opus!' aspice primum,
> quanto cum fastu, quanto molimine circum-

spectemus vacuam Romanis vatibus aedem!
mox etiam, si forte vacas, sequere et procul audi,
quid ferat et quare sibi nectat uterque coronam.
caedimur et totidem plagis consumimus hostem
lento samnites ad lumina prima duello.
discedo Alcaeus puncto illius; ille meo quis?
quis nisi Callimachus? si plus adposcere visus,
fit Mimnermus et optivo cognomine crescit.
multa fero, ut placem genus irritabile vatum,
cum scribo et supplex populi suffragia capto;
idem, finitis studiis et mente recepta,
obdurem patulas impune legentibus aures.
ridentur mala qui componunt carmina; verum
gaudent scribentes et se venerantur et ultro,
si taceas, laudant quidquid scripsere beati.   (87ff.)

*There were two brothers in Rome, one a lawyer, the
other a speech teacher. Their agreement was that each
one should hear nothing but praise from the other's
mouth; one was to be a Gracchus in the other's eyes
and in turn the other was to be Mucius. Doesn't this
madness possess our shrill bards just as much? I write
lyric; he writes elegy. 'Marvellous! A work with the
stamp of the nine Muses!' Note first, with what fas-
tidiousness, with what determination, we look round
Apollo's library with the shelves vacant for Roman
bards! Presently, if you've time, follow and listen outside the door to what either poet brings to the recita-
tion and why he weaves himself his own crown. We
take the blows and give as good as we get to the opponent, like gladiators in a half-hearted contest at dusk.
I leave an Alcaeus by his vote: what's his title by mine?
Nothing less than Callimachus! Or if he seems to want
more, he becomes Mimnermus and grows greater from
the desired title. I put up with a lot to please the
touchy tribe of bards, while I write and modestly seek
some popular esteem. Personally, my poetic career over
and my sanity regained, I would stop my ears, which
readers of their own poetry found open without fear of*

reciprocation. *Bad poets are laughed at; but then they
love their own writing and worship themselves and, if
you are silent, they are not backward in praising whatever they have written, happy in their own conceit.*

It is clear why Horace is fulminating: belonging to the older
generation of Augustan poets and assuming that Fuscus and
his larger public would know that, in fact, he did not indulge
in this mutual back-scratching, as he pretends he does, he could
criticize in this way the poets who wrote for the audiences Ovid
would attract as his poetic production increased. These are, of
course, deductions based on slender evidence, but they make
the Augustan literary scene far more comprehensible than do
the assumptions that Horace and Propertius were somehow
mutual admirers.

Horace, of course, was to hit back more subtly in his fourth
book of *Odes*, which appeared around 15 B.C. To take an example, in the third ode of that book he addresses Melpomene, the
muse of tragic and lyric poetry, although the particular relationships to poetry of the Nine muses were not as yet as fixed as
they were to be later. The important lines are these:

> Romae principis urbium
>> dignatur suboles *inter amabiles*
> *vatum ponere me choros,*
>> et iam dente minus mordeor invido.
> *o, testudinis aureae*
>> *dulcem quae strepitum, Pieri, temperas,*
> *o mutis quoque piscibus*
>> *donatura cycni, si libeat, sonum*
> totum muneris hoc tui est,
>> quod monstror digito praetereuntium
> Romanae fidicen lyrae:
>> quod spiro et placeo, si placeo, tuum est. (*Od.* 4.3.13ff.)

*The offspring of Rome, chief among cities, deigns to put
me* among the lovable choruses of bards *and I am now
less bitten by the tooth of envy. O Pierian Muse,* you
who modulate a sweet strain on the golden tortoise-shell
lyre, and who can give the voice of the swan to dumb

fishes also, *if you wish, it is all due to your gift that I am
pointed out by the fingers of passersby as the minstrel of
the Roman lyre: that I breathe and please, if I do please,
is your doing.*

This is a very clear and hostile allusion to the important
explication of the poet's principles and aspirations that closes
Propertius' second book. There Propertius writes:

> *tale facis carmen docta testudine quale*
> *Cynthius impositis temperat articulis.*
> non tamen haec ulli venient ingrata legenti,
> sive in amore rudis sive peritus erit.
> *nec minor hic animis, ut sit minor ore, canorus*
> *anseris indocto carmine cessit olor.*
> haec quoque perfecto ludebat Iasone Varro,
> Varro Leucadiae maxima flamma suae;
> haec quoque lascivi cantarunt scripta Catulli,
> Lesbia quis ipsa notior est Helena;
> haec etiam docti confessa est pagina Calvi,
> cum caneret miserae funera Quintiliae.
> et modo formosa quam multa Lycoride Gallus
> mortuus inferna vulnera lavit aqua!
> *Cynthia quin vivet versu laudata Properti*
> *hos inter si me ponere Fama volet.* (2.34.79ff.)

You produce a song on the learned tortoise-shell lyre
such as Cynthian Apollo modulates with his fingers on
the strings. *These poems however will not be found
unacceptable to the reader, whether he be inexperi-
enced or skilled in love.* And here too the tuneful swan,
no less proud, though less loud, triumphs over the un-
trained note of the goose. *Such poems Varro also toyed
with when his Jason was finished. Varro the great love
of his Leucadia; such poems sang from the writings of
wanton Catullus, through which Lesbia is better known
than Helen herself. Such poems too the pages of the
erudite Calvus admitted, when he sang of the death of
poor Quintilia. And lately how many wounds from the
beautiful Lycoris did Gallus in death bathe in the waters*

of the underworld! Cynthia too will live, praised in the verse of Propertius, if Fame will be willing to put me among these.

Horace's claim that the rising generation puts him *inter amabiles vatum choros* is a direct challenge to Propertius' ambition of belonging to the select company of the neoterics such as Catullus and Gallus *(hos inter si me ponere Fama volet)*. Horace's reference to the voice of the swan (4.3.20) takes up Propertius' similar references (2.34.84), both perhaps echoing Vergil *(Ecl.* 9.35–6), *videor . . . argutos inter strepere anser olores*, but Horace sarcastically suggests that the Muse could give the voice of the swan even to mute fishes *(mutis quoque piscibus donatura cycni . . sonum).*

Horace also says that he is now less bitten by the fangs of envy. Who might be taken as representative of this envy? In the light of the above and the frequent linguistic allusions in Horace's ode to Propertius' poem *(testudinis aureae/docta testudine; strepitum . . . temperas/carmen . . . temperat; ponere me/me ponere),* can we doubt that the *Romanae fidicen lyrae* is expressing his reciprocal resentment of the Roman Callimachus? Horace is suggesting that the period when he felt threatened is now passed, but that now it is his turn. One may note, incidentally, that, in accordance with common ancient practice, neither mentions the other by name. That, after all, might ensure some sort of literary survival: just as Callimachus attacks the anonymous Telchines and Ovid attacks the unknown Ibis, so Horace and Propertius grapple with each other's pretensions, but the *cognoscenti* have to appreciate the feud through literary allusions without the naming of names: a similar practice may be observed in contemporary classical scholarship.

In ode 6, Horace's boasts get louder. His audience is different from that of Propertius: virgins, young boys and respectable matrons, not lovers and light women.[14] And just as in 2.34.93

14 Cp. Prop. 2.34.81–2 *(sive in amore rudis sive peritus erit);* 3.2.10 *(turba puellarum);* 3.3.20 *(expectans sola puella virum)* with Hor. *Od.* 3.1.4 *(virginibus puerisque canto)* and *Od.* 4.6.31–2 *(virginum primae puerique claris patribus orti).*

Propertius mentioned his own name, so in this ode Horace too inserts his name in the closing line *('docilis modorum vatis Horati').* This is not a common occurrence in either poet.

In ode 7 the reference to Theseus and Pirithous might be taken as accidental, did we not know of the prominent mention of this pair in the opening elegy of Propertius' Book 2. Ode 9 takes as its theme the poverty of the poet and his sole ability to give what the recipient of the poem most wishes – the immortality of song. Horace then treats this gift of song as Propertius treated the gift of song in 3.1. The muse alone confers immortality, says Horace. His list of examples are similar to, although not the same as Propertius' in 3.1, where Propertius says, using an old Hellenistic *topos*, that without poetry Homer, Troy and the heroes connected with it would not even be known to us.[15] Horace makes the same claim in a crisper and more memorable phrase, as Solmsen pointed out:

> vixere fortes ante Agamemnona
> multi; sed omnes illacrimabiles
>   urgentur ignotique longa
>   nocte, carent quia vate sacro.

> *many brave men lived before Agamemnon; but all, un-*
> *wept and unknown, are plunged in the long night, be-*
> *cause they lack a sacred bard.*

A main point is that the poetry conferring this immortality is different, and each poet is claiming that his is the most appropriate vehicle for fame. But more, Horace now entrusts to fame not a Cynthia, as Propertius does, but prominent Romans of the time such as Lollius. He deliberately contrasts his own poetry to that of Propertius by associating himself with Alcaeus, Pindar, Simonides and other lyric poets. He terms these *minaces* or *graves Camenae* (as opposed to any *leves Musae*). This is a deliberate challenge to elegy and perhaps indicates some insecurity about victory in the Callimachean/anti-Callimachean controversy. The *Monobiblos*, after all, had been a greater popular success than the first three books of the *Odes*. To make the

---

15 One notices, however, that Paris, Hector and *Deiphobus* are
   examples common to both.

point even clearer, he claims that even the themes of Anacreon
and Sappho were immortalized by their *lyric* poetry:

> nec, si quid olim *lusit* Anacreon,
> delevit aetas; spirat adhuc amor
> > vivuntque commissi calores
> > > Aeoliae fidibus puellae. (4.9.9–12)

> *Time has not obliterated Anacreon's playful days; the
> love still breathes and the passions still live that were
> entrusted to the strings of the Aeolian girl.*

Some of the poems in this fourth book of *Odes* are deliberately intended to indicate to readers of love poetry that lyric
in its Teian vein could handle the themes of amatory elegy just
as well as Propertius could. Examples are the odes to Ligurinus
(10) and Lyce (13), the latter seeming to invite comparison
with the poems of Propertius that deal with Cynthia's growing
old. In ode 15 Horace takes up the familiar theme of the
recusatio and moves on to the Propertian topic of peace. Horace,
however, makes Augustus the recipient of his compliments for
the establishment of universal peace. We do not find this in
Propertius, and it might seem that Horace is trying to outdo
Propertius by making the god of peace, whom that poet so
constantly honours, Augustus himself. Most, if not all, of Horace's fourth book of *Odes* may be construed as a critical reply
to the upstart Alexandrian Propertius, who was challenging both
Vergil and Horace for the poetic crown. Horace, in my view, is
somewhat on the defensive. It is clear from the enthusiasm and
success of Ovid that the Alexandrians. the poets of private
rather than public themes, were winning the day. Horace could
not anticipate the verdict of history which would leave Vergil
and himself with the bays they both craved and Propertius with
the misunderstanding of centuries.

Poetic materials

It would be regrettable to leave the impression that the Propertian *oeuvre* was devoted solely to muted literary polemic and
discussion of the canons of true poetry. The forces shaping

Propertius' poetry may be left for later discussion, but this is an appropriate point at which to sketch briefly the contents of the surviving books, emphasizing the relative importance to Propertius, at different stages of his poetic career, of his various themes. Naturally, any summary of this type is open to criticism, but it is important to appreciate the *variety* of Propertius' elegies as well as their poetic consistency. What follows is therefore cursory and concentrates on those facets of Propertius which have not been treated at length elsewhere in these pages.

The centrality of his mistress Cynthia in Propertius' work is properly symbolized by the powerful opening elegy of Book 1. The poem is programmatic, more or less summarizing the main body of the poetry that follows. This describes, in poems often addressed to his more important or more literary friends, the agonies of the affair with Cynthia, which he characterizes as having lasted, so far, a year. The mythological *exemplum* he adduces to contrast with his own plight is the story of Milanion, who painfully wooed and finally won Atalanta. The opening lines are a clear imitation, as often, of an Hellenistic model, here Meleager(*A.P.* 12.101). Oddly enough, one of Atalanta's former suitors had been the luckless Meleager of mythology. No doubt this learned allusion was picked up by those who still admired neoteric poetry. Propertius' final advice to more fortunate lovers, to stay with those who treat them well, illustrates the didactic aspect of elegy, which was, in Rome, to reach its peak in Ovid's rhetorical *Ars Amatoria*.

In the elegies that follow, we are given an impressionistic picture of Cynthia's character, the nature of their relationship, and the psychological agonies of Propertius in grappling with Cynthia's coquettishness and infidelity. We see him wrestling with friends who are trying to drag him away from her, with the rivals who try to steal her. Yet he defends his lovesick state and warns those friends who write that one day they will regret that they lack his particular poetic abilities. Once under the sway of love, they too will appreciate not only what he goes through, but the power of his verses and the importance of amatory elegy as a literary *genre,* which can combine utility with art. In elegy 7, addressed to Ponticus, who was presumably the author of an epic *Thebaid,* we first see in Propertius the barbed defensiveness of the elegist which recurs as a theme throughout all the elegists' work; the poet proclaims the importance of elegy, even though it was regarded by the most important Augustan poets (such as Horace) as a trivial – but threatening – form of art. Two typical elegiac subjects drawn from Alexandrian art-forms may be singled out. As noted earlier, elegy 16 is a variation on the *paraclausithyron,* the lament of the lover lying in front of the closed door.[16] Here the door speaks rather than the hapless lover in front of it. Elegy 20 is an elegiac 'epyllion', narrating the story of Hylas' capture by nymphs. Its ostensible occasion is didactic: a warning to Gallus[17] to watch out for his young boyfriend. Elegies 21 and 22 are untypical of the rest of Propertius' work, but here they identify the poet and give the reader information about his origins and some inkling of his political connections. The first is a lament for a relative, also named Gallus, who was killed during the Civil War. He adumbrates Propertius' own anti-war attitudes and the short piece is based upon a common type of funerary epigram, popular in both classical and Alexandrian times. It is a dramatic address to a passerby to take the news of his death home. The last poem of the book gives Propertius' identity.

Book 2 opens as usual with a programmatic elegy, this time addressed to Maecenas. It is generally taken as a sign of his

16 The most convenient discussion of the theme is to be found in F.O. Copley, *Exclusus Amator. A Study in Latin Love Poetry* (Michigan–Oxford 1956); see n. 8 above.
17 Gallus, the name of a friend addressed in three of the elegies of Book 1, is also the name of Propertius' relative who was killed after the siege of Perusia. Traditionally, and frequently by those critics strongly opposed to the biographical approach, it is denied that Propertius' 'friend' can be the C. Cornelius Gallus, the earlier elegist who committed suicide in 26 B.C. under pressure from Augustus and whose death Propertius alludes to at 2.34.91. I see nothing impossible about identifying Propertius' friend Gallus with C. Cornelius. Propertius' youthful presumption of such a friendship, based perhaps on little or no acquaintance (although that cannot be excluded), would conform to Roman conventions for honorific addressees. It would be compatible with his own self-esteem, which emerges even more strongly in his claims to literary fame. The coincidence of name with his relative is awkward but not confusing, and for the sake of laying claim to a 'friendship' with the admired elegist (cf. 2.34.91) Propertius would have tolerated the awkwardness.

gaining admission to that circle, but there are difficulties about this hypothesis. Alluding directly to Callimachus' dictum that it is Jove's right to thunder, not the poet's (Fr. 1 Pf.), Propertius claims that it is because of Cynthia that he writes as he does and that she provides enough themes for his poetry. The whole poem is light and ironic. Propertius declares that had he the talent he would not write standard mythological poetry from the epic cycle, nor even standard historical epic (which might be more acceptable by Callimachean standards), but would sing of the great historical achievements of Augustus and Maecenas' fidelity to him. But since he is in love he cannot escape his fate.

The following poems, up to elegy 10, describe the shifts in Propertius' relationship with Cynthia. They examine his own ambiguous attitudes towards her, the jealousies she occasions, and the triumphs he occasionally manages to achieve. Elegy 7 embodies his own personal protest against the Augustan legislation which would force Propertius to marry and so, in a sense, abandon Cynthia. In elegy 10 he proclaims that he will now give up writing about love and start to write, in the most elevated spirit, a contemporary epic, perhaps about the forthcoming expedition against the Parthians. Elegy 11 is an uncharacteristically short poem expressing, in accord with the tone of elegy 10, one of his bitter withdrawals from Cynthia: others can write about you; may you lie in an unhonoured tomb.

Elegy 12 is an ecphrastic poem, a genre developed by the Alexandrians, although its inspiration goes back to Homer. Such poems purport to describe a real, or even fictitious, painting or sculpture. The tedious epigrams on Myron's cow are perhaps the best known, but it was a frequent form in Roman literature. Propertius certainly used it more than Tibullus. The poet is apparently describing a picture of Love with wings and arrows and explaining the appropriateness of the symbolism. It is with elegy 13ff. that we descry the problems that plague Book 2 and which induce editors, in despair, to begin classifying as complete poems sections which may be simply separated from a larger poem or misplaced. Various transpositions and alternative divisions have been suggested to mend matters, but certain general themes clearly emerge from the extant frag-

ments. Elegy 13 tells how his subjection to love has taught him
not to condemn *tam graciles Musas,* because by his amatory
verse he can impress Cynthia and this is all that he desires.
When he dies, he wants simply to be known as one who has
written a few books of love poetry; for he is love's slave and
death cannot come too early for one in his plight. Elegies 14
and 15 describe one of the few occasions when his affair with
Cynthia is going well. Then he can defend love as something
that should be contrasted with the cruelty of war. Elegies 16,
17, and 18, whatever the divisions agreed on, all deal with hard
times: the duplicity and infidelity of Cynthia. Even a humorous
and playful poem such as 19 expresses the jealousy that figures
prominently in this book. In 20, he contrasts her fickleness with
his own devotion to her. 21ff. explores further, frequently using
the themes of Greek epigram, his own wavering psychology, the
vulnerability of all to love, and he begins now to explain the
sort of fame he has in mind: he will win for Cynthia the glory
that Calvus and Catullus bestowed on their beloved mistresses.
But a didactic note continues to be sounded: what one must
endure if one is a rival for a woman. A note of rescue is sounded
in a dream poem (26a). The occasional triumph is recorded but
always in the context of death. Elegy 27 states specifically the
connection, typical in Roman and romantic poetry, of love and
death – only the lover knows how he will die; soldiers and
sailors do not. Elegy 28 has been divided and transposed in
numerous ways, but it evokes a time when Cynthia was severely
ill and Propertius prayed to the gods of the underworld and
Jupiter for her recovery. A playful tone makes itself heard in
29, although this poem, too, is somewhat controversial in its
arrangement. Propertius runs into a band of Cupids, who drag
him to Cynthia's house. Cynthia accuses *him* of infidelity for a
change. A chord of defensiveness is struck in 30b, where he
defends his love-stricken behaviour by various mythological
parallels. Elegy 31 gives a description of the Temple just dedicated to Apollo and serves ingeniously as an excuse for Propertius'
lateness in visiting Cynthia; in turn, Elegy 33 is a complaint that
Cynthia prefers to stay up and drink rather than go to bed with
him. Elegy 32 reverts to the theme of jealousy, but with a touch
of the complacency that Ovid was later to display.

The final elegy of Book 2, sometimes wrongly divided into two, as was suggested earlier, is a triumphant defence of the writing of amatory poetry and the inevitability of even his most severe critics one day falling in love. The poem opens with a protestation that Lynceus has been trying to steal Cynthia, but Propertius forgives him because now he will understand why all find love desirable. He is delighted that Lynceus can now feel what he has so long felt, for he will now realize that philosophy and the more elevated literary forms are useless here; that the works of Philitas and Callimachus are those to admire, imitate, and read. Propertius advises Lynceus to give up writing on the standard cyclic themes about Troy and Thebes; even Aeschylean tragedy is of no avail. We must now come to grips with your passion, he says, and only by writing like Propertius will you have a chance of affecting the girl's heart. For all Propertius' poverty, he is a sort of king of love. It is at this point there occurs the ambiguous, possibly ironic, reference to Vergil's *Aeneid*.[18]

The purport of the reference is that even the famous Vergil has written pastoral love poetry which, with his Hesiodic *Georgics*, was the type of poetry the neo-Alexandrians could admire. All of these a lover can appreciate and their delicate verse is not to be overshadowed by louder and emptier poetry. Other poets like Varro, Catullus, and last, but by no means least, Gallus, had also written the sort of poetry of which Propertius proudly proclaims himself a master. This is the obverse of the standard *recusatio:* it is the claim that love poetry is, in some ways and for certain people, far more important than the statelier genres preferred by the Augustan establishment. This last elegy of Book 2 is perhaps more defiantly Alexandrian in its verse technique, with 13 polysyllabic pentameter endings in its 94 lines, as well as in its acknowledgement of Callimachean models and followers, because Propertius is showing more bravado in defence of his life and poetry than elsewhere. It is a fitting close to Book 2 and shows more of the developing irony and tension that become increasingly noticeable in his mature work. Interestingly, Propertius does not exclude Gallus from his

18 See above, pp. 24ff.

list of illustrious precursors, despite Gallus' fairly recent suicide in 26 B.C. on Augustus' orders. One may be reading too much anti-Augustanism into his references to Vergil, but the invocation of Gallus is clearly in defiance of the regime.

Book 3 opens with an address to the shades of Callimachus and Philitas. Here Propertius proclaims his originality and his opposition to epic. He boasts that he is a great poet of love and the sort of poetry best read in peace time will bring him appropriate poetic laurels. He contrasts historical epic and the writings that celebrate the Augustan regime and its imperial conquests with his own softer poetry which will one day be appreciated, even if only after his death. Elegy 2 reiterates his claim to fame, despite his poverty, and the immortality he will bestow upon his beloved. It is in this poem that there occurs the critical adaptation, mentioned earlier, of Horace's triumphant close to his three books of *Odes,* published in late 23 B.C. Propertius, following carefully the outlines of Horace's claim, puts in his own claim to immortality. The third poem also alludes to Callimachus and is in the form of a *recusatio.* He imitates the Hesiodic dream used by Callimachus. He was dreaming of writing a book somewhat like the *Aeneid,* perhaps on the kings of Alba and the glories of Roman history, recalling Ennius' *Annales.* But Apollo stops him, warning him that his proper *forte* is love poetry; his genius is not equipped for such lofty themes. And then, amid a wealth of Alexandrian symbolism and imagery[19] he is in the presence of Calliope, who reiterates that his talents are not for martial poetry, but for elegy, the *paraclausithyron* and the didactic poetry which will charm young ladies who wish to deceive their austere husbands and lovers. The final lines present Propertius baptized, as it were, by Calliope in the water of Philitas.

As if to stress this pronounced defiance of the Augustan literary establishment, elegy 4 is an ironic anti-war poem, in which Propertius gives his blessing to expeditions against India and Parthia, but insists that he will only watch the triumph from the side of the road, with his arms around his lady love.

19 For a discussion of the imagery, see G. Luck, *The Latin Love Elegy*[2] (London 1969) 132ff.

If any one poem summarizes Propertius' attitude to Augustan Rome, it is this. Elegy 5, which, with 4, is clearly a diptych, says quite decidedly that the god of peace is Love and lovers revere peace. The only wars they want involve sexual battles in the bedroom. He laments the sufferings that imperialism brings and casts considerable doubt upon the sincerity of his earlier valedictions by stating clearly that after death there is no distinction between victor and vanquished. While he is still young, he wants to write love poetry, and when old he will turn to philosophy. Those who delight in war may bring back the standards of Crassus.

After these five defiant elegies, which express most clearly Propertius' anti-Augustan attitudes, he returns in the poems following to his central themes, Cynthia and Love. A vignette describing a break with Cynthia is followed by a fairly conventional, if ingenious, attack on money in the form of a lament for Paetus. 3.8 is an amusing description of a quarrel with Cynthia. Elegy 9, as we have seen, is a careful and mocking imitation of Horace *Odes* 1.1.

Elegy 10 reverts to Cynthia in an unpretentious birthday poem. Elegy 11 is the puzzling elegy on Cleopatra discussed above (pp. 21ff.). Beneath the surface flattery of Augustus, a disdain for the glory and the heroics of war is clearly visible (57–64). Elegy 12, to Postumus, is also against war and develops further a dominant theme of the first half of the book. Postumus, who is apparently about to embark on a Parthian expedition, is berated for leaving behind his faithful wife, Aelia Galla. Propertius attacks the desire for war and the spoils of war. Under its mythological trappings, it is an impassioned plea.

In 13, Propertius returns to the more traditional motifs of amatory elegy: the decay of morals; the fondness for wealth that ruins the course of true love. He laments the past when all was peaceful and simple, allowing natural instincts to prevail. Elegy 13 generalizes the attitudes of 12 and the next poem elaborates on the theme. Sparta offered a more natural approach to love than the corrupt Rome of Propertius' day. There is no praise here of the Spartan chastity that Plutarch's *Lycurgus* depicts but, rather, the assumption that the simple life of Sparta fostered natural gratification. Elegy 15 is more autobiographical;

it is the first and only reference to his first affair – with Lycinna, Cynthia's maid. It professes his constant love for Cynthia, but also protests her cruelty against her servant. The poem therefore represents the poetic heart of the book, despite the surrounding emphasis on his literary and political attitudes.

Elegy 16 confirms this, but it is a sign of his waning interest in Cynthia, in poetic if not personal terms, that a letter from her summoning him to Tibur is made the occasion not for the circumstantial realism of Books 1 and 2 but for general reflections on the immunity of the lover to all dangers on his way to the beloved (as noted earlier, it is also a barbed thrust at Horace). Elegy 17, which has reminiscences of various Hellenistic epigrams on the subject (e.g. Meleager, *A.P.* 12.49), is a long hymn to wine as a cure for love. Elegy 18 is a somewhat perfunctory tribute to M. Claudius Marcellus who was allegedly drowned in 23 B.C. at Baiae; Propertius manages to combine it with general reflections on death. Elegy 19 deploys the usual mythological *exempla* to assert the greater lustfulness of women as opposed to men. Elegy 20 brings us back to Cynthia. Although she is not named, the references to the moon and Phoebus Apollo (3.20.12, 14) leave little room for doubt; another infidelity[20] is followed by reconciliation.

Elegy 21 reverts to a common theme, touched upon even in 1.1: travel mends a broken heart. (This would not have been Horace's view – *caelum, non animum, mutant qui trans mare currunt.*) It is a break with Cynthia because of her harsh treatment of him. Distance and distraction will provide the cure. This elegy points to the death of the relationship, which will culminate in the last two poems of the book. These express, curtly and bitterly, in terms deliberately reminiscent of Catullus' bitter farewells to Lesbia, Propertius' complete rejection of Cynthia.

The progression is broken, however, by the careful juxtaposition of 3.22, addressed to Tullus, pleading the case of Italy

20 I cannot agree with such commentators as W.A. Camps (*ad loc.*) that these poems refer to some new mistress; *in amore novo* (3.20.16) is not incompatible with a new start after one of Cynthia's infidelities. Cynthia similarly reimposed terms (*foedera, formula legis*) on Propertius in like circumstances (4.8.71ff.).

against any of the wonders abroad; and by the next elegy, a frigid poem, imitated by Ovid, on the loss of his writing tablets which had carried so many important *billets-doux* between his mistress and himself.

Indeed, given the solid and well-arranged opening of the book, the disposition of the closing poems, uneven in quality, is most disappointing. It is difficult not to believe that here, as in our extant Book 2, the ravages of defective textual transmission have played a considerable part. Propertius, as we know from the last elegy of Book 2, the earlier part of Book 3[21] and from Book 4, was moving towards longer elegies in his writing. The brevity of some of the concluding elegies of Book 3 is therefore highly suspect.

Book 4, whether it was edited posthumously, as some believe, or whether it was published by Propertius as his final contribution to elegiac poetry, is a book whose structure bears comparison with Book 1. Many have taken it as his concession to Augustan pressures, his attempt, in poetic forms compatible with Callimachean principles, to produce, finally, something that could be accepted by Maecenas and as a genuine neoteric contribution to Augustan public poetry. Such critics argue that, however few and uninspired the elegies that unite Callimachean aetiological forms with Roman subject matter (2, 4, 9, 10), they are, with his eulogy of Augustus (6), the best he could do to show poetic support of the regime. I shall argue in detail later (see pp. 138ff.), but shall here simply state that this is a mistaken view. True, in the long opening elegy (or diptych) Propertius says boldly, as he frequently has before, that he is about to embark on a new poetic endeavour; in this case, the history of early Rome. As before, he runs through the brave old subjects he may decide to treat and adds (4.1.64) that the treatment of

21 Particularly if we accept the plausible conjunction, suggested by Muretus, Scaliger and others, of elegies 3.1 and 3.2 (yielding 64 lines); 3.4 and 3.5 (yielding 70 lines). Note that 3.3, 3.7 and 3.9 have 52, 72 and 60 lines respectively. Book 1, on the other hand, yields an average of less than 32 lines a poem. The situation may be saved by arguing that Propertius was composing (or arranging) some of his elegies in diptych form, the classical example of which is Ovid's 'Cypassis' diptych (*Am.* 2.7 and 8), but this is a theory which requires careful examination.

these Vergilian themes will be in a Callimachean vein even though the subject is truly patriotic and Roman. Suddenly, however, in lines 71ff., a strange figure, an astrologer, appears, who asserts, as Apollo and Calliope had asserted previously, that Propertius' genius is for amatory elegy only. Nevertheless, the second elegy is aetiological. But it should be noticed, as Hallett has pointed out,[22] that Propertius has chosen an *Etruscan* god, Vertumnus, whose specialty is metamorphosis. The tone is ostensibly light-hearted, but it is scarcely difficult to detect not only his pride in his Umbrian and near-Etruscan origins, but also the underlying criticism of Rome's treatment of one of her oldest allies. This is hardly singing of Roman rituals and gods *(sacra deosque)*[23] or rituals and festivals *(sacra diesque)*, or putting his genius at the service of his country, unless the reader is meant to infer from his deliberately ambiguous use of the word *patria* in lines 60 and 64 that his country is really Etruria and not Rome.

The next elegy, although it is not concerned with Cynthia, whom he had abandoned in Book 3, is a love letter which was to become a model for Ovid's *Heroides* (published probably about A.D. 10). Precious little for Augustus to preen himself on, since it is a reversion to the theme that war should not separate lovers. Arethusa is writing to her husband Lycotas, complaining of his frequent absences on frontier wars. The tone is reminiscent of the Cavalier poet Lovelace. Almost every possible campaign that might have taken place, or did take place, in the implementation of Augustus' frontier policy from 29 B.C. on is mentioned, even the aborted invasion of Britain. The reference to Parthia (35f.) indicates that the poem probably, though not certainly, predated 20 B.C., when the standards of Crassus were recovered through diplomacy and the frequently aired plans for war in that area were quietly – and wisely – dropped,

22 See Judith P. Hallett, *Book IV: Propertius' Recusatio to Augustus and Augustan Ideals* (diss. Harvard 1971) 98ff. For all the political overtones, the form of the poem is Callimachean, a dialogue between a statue and a passerby (cf. e.g. Callimachus Frr. 114, 197 Pf.). H.E. Pillinger, 'Some Callimachean influences on Propertius, Book 4', *HSCP* 73 (1969) 178ff., has some good general observations on this aspect of Book 4.
23 For a discussion of this emendation, see below, p. 138, n.27

as were the allusions to it in Augustan poetry. The Parthians were the 'Red menace' of Augustan propaganda. Arethusa, however, shows no concern at all about patriotism. Propertius resumes his standard attack on war and the grief it causes married couples, putting into Arethusa's mouth a curse against military manufacturers:

> occidat, immerita qui carpsit ab arbore vallum
>   et struxit querulas rauca per ossa tubas. (19–20)

Since some Augustan legislation was aimed at encouraging marriage and births in the interest of social stability, Propertius is perhaps hinting at a contradiction between Augustus' domestic and imperialist policies. Elegy 4 might seem to be a fulfilment of the promise made at the opening of the book. It is a poetic discussion of the places associated with the traitress Tarpeia. But what do we find in the treatment? An emotionally incoherent juxtaposition of official and private attitudes. The main interest centres on Tarpeia's love for the besieger of Rome; the more usual version of the story stressed her venality. Her condemnation is somewhat perfunctory, and we cannot say that this episode in Roman history was one of the great triumphs to which an Augustan poet might profitably allude. Elegy 5 is typical of Alexandrian amatory themes, a playfully vituperative poem on a procuress, a theme familiar to us from Herodas and recapitulated by Tibullus and Ovid. Perhaps elegy 6, then, celebrating the Battle of Actium, is the poem intended to make good his new programme. This notorious poem, beginning with apparent solemnity: *sacra facit vates,* has been described by Gordon Williams as 'one of the most ridiculous poems in the Latin language'.[24] Elegy 7 returns, as the sceptical critic of Propertius might expect, to the subject which the astrologer Horos (in 4.1) had insisted alone suited his talent. It is the moving, and mysterious, elegy on Cynthia's apparition. Elegy 8, his humorous *chef d'oeuvre,* deals with an episode in his long and varied love affair with Cynthia.

Perhaps elegy 9, then, moves nearer to the new poetic mode

---

24 *JRS* 52 (1962) 43. The problems presented by this elegy are discussed in chapter 4, pp. 144ff.

proclaimed at the opening of the book. Hardly. The poem, explaining the origins of the religious rule that women be excluded from the worship of Hercules at the Ara Maxima, is very Callimachean in its imitation of the Alexandrian poet's mixture of solemnity and humour in his *Hymns*. It manages to allude to Vergil's treatment of the hero in *Aeneid* 8, but Propertius introduces a humour which would be beyond the capacity, or even desire, of Vergil and, in effect, implicitly criticizes Vergil's epic approach to aetiology. Particularly noticeable is the gentle fun Propertius pokes at Hercules in having him speak of performing common household tasks and wearing the Roman equivalent of a brassière:

> 'idem ego Sidonia feci servilia palla
> officia et Lydo pensa diurna colo,
> mollis et hirsutum cepit mihi fascia pectus,
> et manibus duris apta puella fui.'

Propertius' Hercules is not the Hercules of Book 8 of the *Aeneid* but rather the Hercules of Euripides' *Alcestis* or, indeed, the view of Hercules which Callimachus puts forward in his accounts of Heracles in the first book of the *Aetia* (Frr. 22–3; 24–5 Pf.). If the contemporary interest in the Ara Maxima on the part of the Augustan elite was taken as the occasion for this poem, this might be a further indication of Propertius' ironic attitudes to the Augustan establishment. There is little in it that would appeal to those who would glorify Roman institutions. On the contrary, some of the humour might, in fact, offend those who later in 9 B.C. would be duly impressed by the pomp and ceremony of the dedication of the Ara Pacis Augustae.

Elegy 10 comes nearest to fulfilling the boast Propertius had made in the opening lines of Book 4. It is a somewhat compressed, somewhat perfunctory, and perhaps ironic examination of the three occasions on which the *spolia opima* were won. These were dedicated in the temple of Jupiter Feretrius by the victorious commander who had killed in battle, with his own hand, the opposing general. We know, however, that this topic was very controversial at this period. In 29 B.C. Marcus Licinius Crassus as pro-consul had slain Deldo, king of the Bastarnae, in

single combat and there was a question whether he could dedi-
cate the *spolia opima* in the temple of Jupiter and so become
the fourth Roman general to achieve this great honour. It was,
however, decided (see Dio Cassius 51.24) that he was simply
standing in for Augustus and not supreme commander in his
own right. Once more Propertius, under the guise of good intentions, has introduced material embarrassing to Augustus into
his poetry. To make matters worse, he doctors the standard
historical account. According to Livy (4.18–20), Tolumnius was
killed by A. Cornelius Cossus at Fidenae in 432 B.C. Much
in the style of Sir Walter Scott, the military tribune curses this
violator of treaties and international law (*'ruptor foederis hu-
mani violatorque gentium iuris'*) and cuts him down on the
battlefield. Propertius, however, with his Etruscan bias, places
Tolumnius' death at Veii, where the Romans were clearly the
aggressors,[25] and adds a poignant lament for the departed
glories of that city (27–30).

The famous elegy on Cornelia, which concludes the book,
might be taken as an elegiac hymn to the virtues of Roman
womanhood, which Augustus was trying to restore. And yet
Cornelia stands for everything that Propertius, to judge from his
previous poetry, has not been able to tolerate in a woman.[26]
The poem may be taken as a somewhat frigid tribute to a
friend or, rather, his wife, but there is in it none of the poetic
ebullience and feeling that show themselves in the poems devoted to Cynthia. Those who hoped that Propertius might become a poetic supporter of the Augustan imperial or moral
regime, the elegiac equivalent of Horace and Vergil, would
find cold comfort in this admired (*regina elegiarum!*), but rarely
examined, poem.

Book 4, as we shall see later, is Propertius' most subtle response
to 'what the age demanded'. Propertius had boasted before, in
the opening elegy of Book 3, of his claim to be the most original and leading representative of Callimachean poetry in Augustan Rome. Book 4 represents the justification of this claim

25 See R. Lucot, 'Problèmes de création chez Properce', *Pallas* 10
(1961) 59–68.
26 See J.P. Hallett, 'The role of women in Roman elegy', *Arethusa*
6 (1973) 119–20.

by displaying the range of Callimachean imitation and influence as well as Propertius' own contribution to that Alexandrian tradition. He displays his technical mastery of Callimachean aetiology, but he exudes, in the few examples of the genre he offers us, hostility to the military establishment. The best poems in the book are on Cynthia, the theme that had been for so long the ostensible core of his work. Only those who find the later books of the *Metamorphoses* of Ovid honest and sincere tributes to the Julian house will find in this last book of Propertius a concession to the regime from which he had found himself increasingly alienated. He may have had to pass on the torch of his hostility to younger, more forthright, or less sensitive, poets such as Ovid. Propertius, whenever he died, clearly did not pay the price that Ovid was to pay for continuance in the Callimachean tradition which had, by this time, become partly a symbol of political opposition.

Later life

Little is known about Propertius' life other than what can be cautiously reconstructed from his own writings and fragmentary evidence in other authors. Suetonius' *Lives of the Poets*, had the work survived, might have been helpful. Speculation therefore thrives.

In private life, the break with Cynthia, bitterly recorded in the last elegy of Book 3, and conventionally dated to around 24 B.C., may not have been final. The relationship has been variously estimated at five, seven, and even ten years' duration. Whatever and whenever its final end, Cynthia's ghost (4.7) claims that she was replaced in Propertius' affections by a certain Chloris (4.7.72) whom she describes as a common harlot (4.7.39), a description which, of course, is scarcely to be taken more seriously than the rest of the 'evidence' in that evocative poem. If her ghost were to be believed, she died poor, in very suspicious circumstances, and was buried at Tibur (4.7.85).

One may assume that Propertius was dead by 1 B.C. Ovid's reference to Propertius, when speaking of past poets (*A.A.* 333, 536) would be most unpropitious, were he not. The *Ars Amatoria*, an amusing parody of erotic elegy, which may have to take partial responsibility for its decline, is plausibly dated to shortly after 1 B.C. But did Propertius die long before this? The sixth and eleventh elegies of Book 4 may be dated to after 16 B.C.;[27] possibly the timeliness of these poems would prompt the speedy publication of the book in 15 B.C. The rest of the material suggests that this book was Propertius' swan song, or that it was published by editor(s) posthumously. The artistic arrangement and underlying poetic principles certainly indicate either Propertius' own hand or an excellent editor. I prefer to believe that Propertius was responsible for Book 4 and that thereafter he abandoned elegiac poetry to such younger competitors and admirers as Ovid.

The question still remains in which of the thirteen years following did Propertius die? We must ignore, of course, his poetic descriptions of his physical state, which might be modelled on the Alexandrian equivalents of 'Why so pale and wan, fond lover?' Pliny the Younger however supplies some further evidence. In writing of his friend, the learned Roman knight Passennus Paulus, himself an elegist, and born at Assisi, he twice insists that Passennus was a *descendant* of Propertius, as well as an admirer and imitator of his poetry (*Ep.* 6.15.1; 9.22.1). This may indicate that Propertius ultimately married, had a child or children, perhaps after returning to his birthplace, and lived longer than the standard biographies allow. The instances of poets burning out their youthful talents are as numerous as the examples of successful poets developing late in life. Propertius, to judge from Book 4, at least went out with a flourish.

Poetic reputation

After Ovid's praise, and his extensive imitation of him, not only in the *Amores* and *Ars Amatoria*, but also in the *Heroides* and *Fasti*, allusions and references to Propertius in ancient literature are comparatively few. Martial claims that Cynthia made him

27 Propertius refers (4.6.77) to the subjugation of the Sygambri, which would be after the minor defeat of M. Lollius in Gaul by German raiders in 16 B.C., when a legion lost its eagle (Suet. *Aug.* 23; Dio Cassius 54.20). Cornelia died the year her brother, Cornelius Scipio, was consul, 16 B.C. This was also the year in which a four-yearly celebration of Augustus' principate took place.

a poet (*Cynthia te vatem fecit, lascive Properti,* 8.73.5) and we
have already examined the implications of 14.189, *Cynthia –
facundi carmen iuvenale Properti.*

The description seems at least to indicate that the *Monobiblos*
was the work that was best known and circulated after his
death. Juvenal refers in passing to Propertius, and although the
context of the satire on women (6.7) makes it natural that he
should refer only to Cynthia, he makes a witty allusion to 4.7
in satire 2.149ff. Even before this there are Propertian borrow-
ings in the *Copa,* Manilius, Calpurnius Siculus, Lucan, Petronius,
Valerius Flaccus, Statius, Silius Italicus, and a *graffito* of Pompeii.[28] After Juvenal there was a revival of interest in him
with Nemesianus and Ausonius, which continued till the time
of Venantius Fortunatus. Claudian's poem on the Rape of Pros-
erpina, in particular, echoes several passages of Propertius.

In his summary of correct first-century Roman opinion on
literature Quintilian says of the elegists (10.1.93):

> Elegia quoque Graecos provocamus, cuius mihi tersus
> atque elegans maxime videtur auctor Tibullus. Sunt qui
> Propertium malint. Ovidius utroque lascivior, sicut dur-
> ior Gallus.

> *In elegy also we challenge the Greeks, as a writer of
> which Tibullus seems to me the most polished and
> stylish. Some prefer Propertius. Ovid is more sexual
> than either, just as Gallus is harsher.*

This is the last specific reference to him that we have for some
centuries. Propertius had nothing to offer the Middle Ages in
the way, for example, both Vergil the Magician and, at least in
quotation, Juvenal the Moralist had. He was known and he
survived, but any real understanding of his literary value seems
to have vanished in the centuries that followed the decline of
Rome. Similarly his main Alexandrian and Roman models suffered badly in the transmission of classical antiquity to the
Middle Ages. Even with the revival of learning, Propertius,

28 E. Diehl, *Pompeianische Wandinschriften* (Berlin 1930) 785. For
a collection of the literary references, see P.J. Enk, *Sex. Propertii
elegiarum liber I* (*Monobiblos*) (Leiden 1946) 54–76.

because of his difficulty, did not come back into fashion even in the way Petronius did. His successor and imitator, Ovid, because of the very diversity of his work, and the simplicity of his Alexandrianism, fared far better. Ovid's storytelling power, his vulgarization of Propertian motifs, made him, for the late Middle Ages, an easier author to comprehend and also to misunderstand. His rhetorical, linear development of traditional themes of elegy made him far more acceptable to these generations than did the oblique, allusive, and elliptical art of Propertius. The rhetorical facility, almost vulgarity, of Ovid, in certain parts of his work effectively replaced Propertius and, to some extent, Tibullus, even for those who might have had an affinity for Roman love elegy. Perhaps only Catullus, with his directness, stood a chance against the all-pervasiveness of the Ovidian achievement.

The revival of learning naturally saw the production of texts of Propertius and the other elegists. The omnivorous and undiscriminating desire to recover all that could be known and published of the classical heritage helped the survival of even such difficult and misunderstood poets as Propertius. The *editio princeps* was published in 1472 in Venice, along with the work of Catullus, Tibullus and Statius.

Petrarch (1304–74) stands out as the first humanist who went beyond Ovid and took an interest in Propertius, which shows in his work. For example, the sonnet *Solo e pensoso* (1.35), as Wilkins has remarked, is based on Propertius 1.18, an uncharacteristic elegy, which may well have been influenced by Vergil's *Eclogue* 10, where Gallus laments his lost Lycoris amid the inhospitable terrain of Arcadia.[29] The Italian poet, unlike the urban Propertius, could do no more with the theme, but the allusions and adaptations reveal a closer study of the Propertian poem that attracted him than one might expect. Petrarch here seems to have gone beyond his normal Ovidian sources. Our earliest surviving manuscript is the Codex Neapolitanus which was written probably in the twelfth century, perhaps in Germany. One manuscript, however, the Codex Laurentianus, now at Florence, seems to have been written at the end of the four-

29 See E.H. Wilkins, *The Making of the 'Canzoniere' and Other Petrarchan Studies* (Rome 1951) 295–8.

teenth, or the beginning of the fifteenth century, and belonged to Coluccio Salutati, a well-known Florentine statesman, who died in 1406. In 1374, he had written that he would like to acquire a manuscript of Propertius from the library of Petrarch. This manuscript may be a copy of the manuscript Petrarch owned. The younger Burmann duly compiled a *variorum* edition which was completed after his death by Laurentius Santenius and saw the light of day in 1780. This summarized most of the textual emendations and notes that had appeared in thirty or so editions after the *editio princeps*.

The great age of Propertian scholarship came in 1816 with Lachmann, who first began the scientific treatment of Propertius' text. He was followed by Keil (1843), Haupt (1854), Heimreich (1863), Rossberg (1877), and Baehrens (1877). With Lachmann we come into the modern age of Propertian scholarship. There is no space here to record the many attempts (on individual points or in general) to produce a satisfactory text of Propertius. It was a great pity that A. E. Housman did not, because of his personal doubts, continue with an author he found so congenial, but whose problems did not bring out the best of his wayward talents.

Two main directions of scholarship may be noted. One is the belief in wholesale corruption, transposition, and interpolation, and the other a willingness to believe in the obscure, careless, and emotional qualities of Propertius' own writings. Given the artistry of Books 1 and 4, and a better understanding of Propertius' poetics in the light of his Alexandrian predecessors, this second hypothesis must be handled with considerable care. Although radical redivision of the elegies and radical transpositions of lines have been suggested by such critics as O. L. Richmond, it is probably better to approach the problem pragmatically and cautiously. A firm understanding of the nature of Propertius' art seems to be a necessary prerequisite for any future editor of Propertius and a good edition of Propertius is an acknowledged *desideratum*.

The literary criticism and appreciation of Propertius in the nineteenth century tended to centre around critical editions and work on the text. What was said in these contexts tended to be of very dubious quality. As was noted above, there is more merit than is currently allowed in Lachmann's suggestion that Propertius should be credited with five, rather than four, books of poetry. I cannot however sympathize with his attempt to reconstruct the course of Propertius' affair with Cynthia and other details of his life from the evidence of the elegies. The ingenuity seen in his textual work is misplaced in the service of the biographical fallacy. Likewise, one must be sceptical of those critics who, in defending the texts, have been willing to attribute to Propertius more than his share of carelessness, inconsistency, and obscurity. One must be equally sceptical of those who believe that a few mechanical transpositions will uncover a perfect structure in Propertius' Books 2 and 3 and so make sense of the extant *oeuvre*.

It is clear that in the nineteenth century, as is evident from the *obiter dicta* of the commentaries and from the translations produced during the period, a real understanding of Propertius' art was far to seek. True, Propertius found in diverse times and places unexpected defenders and admirers. One such was Vincenzo Padula (1819–93), who wrote and published in 1871 a dissertation on Propertius entitled: *Pauca Quae in Sexto Aurelio Propertio Vincentius Padula Ab Acrio Animadvertebat*. This offered perhaps an overly enthusiastic and romantic view of Propertius, but some of the defences Padula offered against the charges of obscurity and insincerity anticipate modern critical positions.[30]

Nevertheless, if one constructed a collage of late nineteenth- and twentiety-century conventional critical opinion, it would run somewhat as follows:

> 'In Propertius one is conscious of a type of unreserved absorption in love and intense sincerity in its expression' (Duff, p. 415); 'he is a poet of passion rather than reason' (Butler, p. 9); 'He was for a long time spoken of as a writer whose poetry was overlaid and whose passion was chilled by a pedantic display of learning' (Sellar, p. 263); 'Learning affects him for good and for bad. It conduces to his elaborate variegated style . . .

30 See P. V. Tomaszuk, *A Romantic Interpretation of Propertius: Vincenzo Padula* (Aquila 1971).

But it also conduces to stiffness and artificiality . . . Perhaps it is on first acquaintance with Propertius that this conventional side strikes one most: the recondite Alexandrian seems oppressive' (Duff, pp. 420–1). Propertius was 'one of the most intelligent, sophisticated, and eccentric of all Roman poets' (Highet, p. 82), but he had a 'blend of strong sexual passion with something like puritanism' (Highet, p. 87). On the one hand, 'his antiquarianism yielded little fruit . . . Propertius indeed judged rightly in declaring his *forte* to be love, not epic' (Duff, p. 418), but on the other hand, 'He began to see the hollowness of a life devoted to sensuality, its fragmentation and its waste. In his later volumes, he produced poems which were more than personal adventures decorated with mythological allusions. He thought of the past and the future. He created visions of the prehistory of Rome, brilliant etchings worthy to be put near the huge canvas of the *Aeneid*' (Highet, p. 109). 'The tone of his poetry varies greatly: from sensual passion to dull, morbid melancholy; from tongue-in-cheek whimsy to . . . mythological shorthand' (Musurillo, p. 115).

One source informs us that Propertius' first book 'has a freshness and charm which is all its own. Books 2 and 3 are likewise concerned with his love. But the first ecstasy is gone . . . his later work has a harder and more mannered brilliance; but loss of freshness in feeling and colour is compensated by increased strength, incisiveness, and . . . imagination as well' (Barber, p. 737). The most recent standard assessment still has signs of critical incoherence:

> 'Book 1 . . . consists almost entirely of love poems of remarkable grace and wit. This style is maintained in Book 2, though Propertius' association with Maecenas produces as well some elegant tributes to the new regime. Book 3 shows a greater diversity of tone and subject matter . . . the opening poems, which deal with his own poetic position, are among its most successful. Some of the Cynthia poems . . . show his old comic

power, but others are tedious failures . . . In many poems he is attempting to widen his range, but he shows some uncertainty, some crassness, and some lack of assurance in his new style. Book 4 is considerably more successful. It consists partly of the fragments of a Roman *Aetia*, which showed the way to Ovid's *Fasti* . . . To these are added poems on various subjects . . . Polish and refinement are conspicuous in many of his poems . . . In wit, objectivity, and dramatic power and in the thrusting, progressive movement of individual poems he reminds the English reader of John Donne. His obscurity . . . is also like Donne's: much that is puzzling at first becomes plain enough when the implied setting and dramatic development are grasped . . . Propertius' elaborate and self-conscious artistry, his vivid visual and tactile imagination, and his success in integrating what he derives from Greek literature with Roman feeling and Roman life make him one of the most continuously fascinating of the Roman poets.' (Hubbard, p. 886)[31]

Some dissident critical voices, outside classical circles, to be sure, made themselves heard. The *littérateur*, Julien Benda, for example, wrote an interesting, if impressionistic, sketch on Propertius entitled: *Properce ou les amants de Tibur*, which was published in Paris in 1928. Benda's book was interesting because he stressed the Alexandrian artistry of Propertius, playing down the normal assessment of him as a melancholy and obscure love poet. Nevertheless, twentieth-century Propertian studies, were it not for one critical event, would have had to be characterized by their caution. Scholars continued to purge the text of its many errors through emendations and transposition. The expli-

---

31 The works I have used for this compilation (not chosen in all cases for their merits) are: H.E. Butler, *Sexti Properti Opera Omnia* (London 1905); J. Wight Duff, *A Literary History of Rome, From the Origins to the Close of the Golden Age*² (London 1960); G. Highet, *Poets in a Landscape* (Pelican Books 1959); H. Musurillo, *Symbol and Myth in Ancient Poetry* (New York 1961); W.Y. Sellar, *The Roman Poets of the Augustan Age* (Oxford 1899), and the *Oxford Classical Dictionary* (Oxford 1949), *s.v.* 'Propertius' (E.A. Barber), and *OCD*² (Oxford 1970), *s.v.* 'Propertius' (M.H. Hubbard).

cation of individual poems and passages became, as in many
other areas, almost an industry. Themes and *topoi* were, and
continue to be, analysed *ad nauseam* in German and American
dissertations.

Sed quod pace legas . . . Just as Goethe in the eighteenth
century in the *Römische Elegien* seems to show more genuine
appreciation of Propertius than many professional students of
the Classics, so Ezra Pound's notorious *Homage to Sextus Propertius*, completed in 1917, constituted the first genuine critical
advance in the study of Propertius. An account of this work,
part-translation, part-criticism, part-*persona*, has been given
elsewhere.[32] Since that time, in addition to inspiring other
translations of Propertius, as well as such imitations as Robert
Lowell's 'The Ghost', Pound has been largely responsible for
stimulating a lively discussion of the nature of Propertius' art
among a few students of Propertius. It must be confessed,
however, that just as most recent translators (e.g. A. E. Walls,
Constance Carrier, Ronald Musker, J. P. McCulloch, and John
Warden) have not had the desire or the ability to carry over the
newer critical insights into their versions, so too most scholarly
work on Propertius has proceeded along conventional lines.

32 See my *Ezra Pound and Sextus Propertius: A Study in Creative
Translation* (Austin, Texas 1964; London 1965) 3–16. It was, after
all, Pound who first claimed that 'S.P. is tying blue ribbon in the
tails of Virgil and Horace.' *The Letters of Ezra Pound*, ed.
D.D. Paige (New York 1950; London 1954) 91.

2
THE POLITICS OF ELEGY

Elegiac attitudes

We sometimes regret that the Romans were not interested in some of the subjects that interest us or, at least, in the *way* that they interest us. The Romans were interested in money, but not in economics; they were interested in literature, but not interested in literary criticism. On the other hand, *we* are interested in oratory, but not in rhetorical theory; we are interested in free speech, but less so in the varied and complex, sometimes devious, forms free speech must take in differing political and social circumstances. Just as the Romans usually fail to supply us with proper statistics for our economic analyses, so sometimes, in other areas, we are not as aware as we should be of subtle techniques of dissent and criticism which are necessitated by political situations very different from our own. We therefore may be guilty of injustice, literary and moral injustice, to certain writers who do not fit our own paradigms of frankness and free expression. With Roman satire, for example, it is unrealistic to expect the savage and specific political criticisms of Lucilius in the work of Horace, Persius, or Juvenal. Extant Augustan literature offers nothing comparable to the obscene directness of Catullus' criticism of contemporary politicians and officials such as Julius Caesar, P. Sestius, and C. Memmius.

As a corollary to this, it may well be that we, along with other generations, in our admiration for the directness and frankness of such classics as Aristophanes and Catullus have scanted the credit we allow to other poets who, in the nature of things, literary, social, and political, could not possibly imitate such forthrightness and who had therefore to cultivate different, perhaps more subtle, virtues and attitudes in their work.

54

There is a tendency among students of the Augustan age to discuss the literature and the history of the period separately. There are dangers in this, particularly, for students of literature. The historian is acutely aware of the gory paths Octavian trod to reach his ascendancy; of the discomfort he felt about his earlier constitutional arrangements; of the plots against him; of his tub-thumping, but ultimately cautious, policy towards Parthia; and of the intermittent softening and hardening of his attitude towards dissent. The literary critic, on the other hand, in his modern, and in many ways proper, regard for the work of art as a thing in itself, the final focus of his attention, may run into certain avoidable difficulties of interpretation if he ignores the approximate dating of different works by the major Augustan writers. An apparent inconsistency of attitude may sometimes be explained by the difference of times and circumstances. In this respect, Augustan literature is somewhat akin to Soviet literature in the twentieth century. And it is particularly important that we should not assume that Roman poets were any more politically naive than modern Soviet writers are, or than their educated Roman contemporaries were. They were *not* deceived by the constitutional masks thrown over the realities of power. Why else the conspiracies and the nostalgic literature about the Republic and its heroes, such as Cato, Cicero, and Pompey? Surely, if these poets are so admirable and so durable in other ways, it is fairer to look for intelligence in their handling of controversial issues in their works than for naivety or crassness. As Jorge Luis Borges has said: 'A dictatorship is good for writers. Censorship challenges them to make their points with ever greater care and subtlety.'

In discussing the elegists *vis-à-vis* the other Augustan poets, there is no obvious way of distinguishing entirely between personal predilections, literary principles and conventions, and politics proper; these tend to overlap and reinforce one another – just as they do in certain modern literatures. The fairly close relationships that existed in this small city of Rome between the various writers of different persuasions will often blur the distinctions. Horace, the evidence indicates, disliked Propertius and was friendly towards Tibullus; Vergil was close to Gallus; and Propertius, overtly at least, admired both elegists. But, as we know from the case of Hemingway and Scott Fitzgerald, even personal friendship does not entail uncritical attitudes among writers.

If I may go over ground covered earlier, with a different emphasis, I would like to illustrate the surface ambiguity of elegiac attitudes, particularly in the case of Propertius, and I would take first the subject of peace. It is generally thought that the elegists, like the U.S. Air Force, might well have taken for their motto: 'Peace is our profession'. Certainly in elegy 1.10 Tibullus attacks war, praises the benefits of peace and ends with this appeal:

> at nobis, pax alma, veni spicamque teneto
>   profluat et pomis candidus ante sinus   (67–8)

> *Come to us, Kindly Peace; bring the ears of grain and let apples pour forth from your bright bosom.*

Yet in the opening elegy of Book 2, he compliments Messala, his friend and patron, on his victories in Aquitania:

> gentis Aquitanae celeber Messala triumphis   (33).

Indeed, if we can believe the anonymous life, he served with Messala in the Aquitanian war of 31 B.C. and was suitably rewarded. Of course, when he is at death's door in 30 B.C. and Messala is sailing off to Cilicia, he has to praise the Golden Age when all was peaceful:

> non acies, non ira fuit, non bella, nec ensem
>   immiti saevus duxerat arte faber.   (1.3.47–8)

> *There were no battle lines, no atrocities, no wars, and the cruel armourer had not yet grimly fashioned swords.*

There is, on the one hand, a rejection of war and conquest, but on the other a very Roman acceptance of these as necessary, indeed glorious, modes of existence. So in proclaiming a preference for making love, not war, the elegist must self-consciously set himself at odds with the premises of his society, even though he cannot become a radical dissenter disrupting the military machine.

With Propertius, this ambiguity is even more complex and it

is one of several reasons for the opaqueness and the detectable irony in many of his poems. Propertius, after the publication of Book 1, had some connections with the circle of Maecenas, Augustus' right-hand man and his minister of state for domestic affairs. Yet quite apart from the conventional elegiac preference for love rather than war, Propertius had his own personal reasons for his anti-militaristic stance. His family, after all, had been on the wrong side in the Civil War; family property had been confiscated (4.1.129–30); and he had lost at least one relative in the aftermath of the siege of Perusia in 41 B.C. (1.22.7–8). He speaks out specifically and bitterly against war, and particularly against civil strife. There are the conventional protestations about the poet's unfitness for military glory and the lover's reverence for peace:

> non ego sum laudi, non natus idoneus armis (1.6.29)

and

> Pacis Amor deus est, pacem veneramur amantes (3.5.1).

These demurrers, of course, fall far short of '*Hell No, We Won't Go*', the cry of those of draft age in America who were against the Vietnam War, but Propertius developed other personal and more ironic ways of expressing his dissent. Firstly, he has an insistent way of referring adversely to incidents in the Civil War that Augustus would have, presumably, far rather forgotten. In the *sigillum* of Book 1, for instance, he asks Tullus if the tombs of his home of Perusia are known to him, the pyres of those dark days for Italy when civil war drove out Rome's own citizens:

> si Perusina tibi patriae sunt nota sepulchra,
>   Italiae duris funera temporibus,
> cum Romana suos egit discordia cives. (1.22.3–5)

In the middle of the opening poem of the second book he claims that were he not a love poet he would be a writer of contemporary epic (like Cornelius Severus) and would celebrate Augustus' wartime exploits, but, most untactfully, he then alludes to the more painful episodes of the Civil War, to Mutina, to Philippi, and, not least and once again, to the Perusine War, when he refers to the overturned hearths of the ancient Etruscan race:

> eversosque focos antiquae gentis Etruscae.   (1.2.29)

Even Actium, which was to Horace something to celebrate in a great victory ode, is for Propertius an occasion for regretful moralizing. If everyone lived, like Propertius, a life of wine, woman, and song, then there would be no cruel steel, no men-of-war, the sea off Actium would not be rolling Roman bones, and Rome would not be tired of mourning, besieged on every hand by triumphs over her very own people:

> qualem si cuncti cuperent decurrere vitam
>   et pressi multo membra iacere mero,
> non ferrum crudele neque esset bellica navis
>   nec nostra Actiacum verteret ossa mare,
> nec totiens propriis circum oppugnata triumphis
>   lassa foret crines solvere Roma suos.   (2.15.41–6)

Secondly, towards imperial conquest and further wars, which were so much in the air at the time of his writing, Propertius' attitude is again subtly but unmistakably critical. Parthian, Persian, Arabic, or even British expeditions are for Horace opportunities for adulation, boasting, or at very least adventures that offer a welcome alternative to civil war (cf. *Od.* 1.12.53–6; 1.35.29–32, 37–40; 2.9.18–24; 3.3.42–8; 3.5.2–4). Propertius however dismisses such exhortatory or celebratory poetry:

> a valeat, Phoebum quicumque moratur in armis   (3.1.7)

and adds that there will be many to sing Rome's praises in poetic annals and proclaim that Bactria will be the boundary of the empire, but he himself is offering something one can read in *peace time:*

> multi, Roma, tuas laudes annalibus addent,
>   qui finem imperii Bactra futura canent.
> sed, *quod pace legas*, opus hoc de monte sororum
>   detulit intacta pagina nostra via.   (3.1.15–18)

As for that very sore point with the Romans, the standards of Crassus, Propertius is almost flippant about them; his poem on

Caesar's proposed expedition to the Indies begins with an impressive description of his possible territorial and financial acquisitions. Propertius offers a hasty prayer for its success:

> omina fausta cano. Crassos clademque piate!
>   ite et Romanae consulite historiae. (3.4.9–10)

But the whole patriotic effect is undercut when we learn that Propertius, leaning on his girl-friend's arm, will be merely *watching* the triumph, with its lists of captured cities, the Parthian bows and arrows, and the captive captains, from the side of the Sacred Way:

> inque sinu carae nixus spectare puellae
>   incipiam et titulis oppida capta legam,
> tela fugacis equi et bracati militis arcus
>   et subter captos arma sedere duces.

A further proof that his celebration of Augustus' military adventures is not seriously meant is that the next poem in the collection announces that Love is the God of peace:

> Pacis Amor deus est. pacem veneramur amantes. (3.5.1)

Moreover, it is in this poem that we find the most poignant general criticism of what Augustus is doing:

> nunc maris in tantum vento iactamur, et hostem
>   quaerimus, atque armis nectimus arma nova.
> haud ullas portabis opes Acherontis ad undas:
>   nudus in inferna, stulte, vehere rate.
> victor cum victo pariter miscetur in umbris:
>   consule cum Mario, capte Iugurtha, sedes.
>   (3.5.11–16)

This we may paraphrase as:

> *Now we are tossed by the wind against a great sea [i.e., because of our passion for wealth]; we even seek out enemies to conquer; and we take on further wars. You'll carry no wealth with you to the river of Acheron; you'll ride, you fool, naked on the infernal ferry. The conqueror is jumbled in with the conquered among the*

shades: captive Jugurtha sits with the consul Marius who captured him.

Then the concluding lines of the poem expressly nullify Propertius' early prayer for Augustus' success. After a life of love and wine, he says, he'll turn to philosophy; this is how his life will end; let those who prefer war bring home the standards of Crassus:

> exitus hic vitae superest mihi; vos, quibus arma
> grata magis, Crassi signa referte domum.   (3.5.47–8)

Anything further from Horace's *dulce et decorum est pro patria mori* can hardly be imagined. The general irony and attitude is reminiscent of Arthur Hugh Clough's lines in *Amours de Voyage:*

> *Dulce* it is, and *decorum*, no doubt, for the country to
>   fall, — to
> Offer one's blood an oblation to Freedom, and die for
>   the Cause, yet
> Still, individual culture is also something, and no man
> Finds quite distinct the assurance that he of all others
>   is called on,
> Or would be justified even, in taking away from the
>   world that
> Precious creature, himself.   (2.2.1–6)

It is this persistent strain of criticism, expressed in various modes of irony, indirection, humour, pathos, and elegiac complaint throughout the first three books, which casts doubt on the traditional theory of Propertius' conversion in Book 4 to Augustan ideals, particularly in the elegiac hymn celebrating Actium (4.6). The features of that puzzling book are, we shall see, open to a different explanation. Propertius, like Horace and Vergil, and unlike Tibullus and Ovid, may have been in a difficult position. He had some tenuous connection at some time with Maecenas' circle, but his literary principles and apparently his general social and political views seem radically different. This would have an effect on his poetry and will account partly for its allusive, elliptical, and sometimes difficult and ambiguous

character. Like Horace in his *Satires* and like Vergil throughout his work, Propertius must have been subject to various sorts
of social and personal pressure, which have left their mark on
his poetry.

Ovid's debt to Propertius

It is perhaps illuminating to compare Propertius' indirectness
with that of his successor. Ovid's attitude to the bellicose spirit
of the time is typically ingenious. On the one hand, he makes
the claim that the life of adulterous leisure *(otium)* is as strenuous as that of the warrior:

> militat omnis amans, et habet sua castra Cupido.
> *(Am.* 1.9.1)

On the other hand, the life of love and elegiac poetry secures
immortal fame as the dusty rewards of military life do *not*
(praemia militiae pulverulenta, Am. 1.15.1–8). But it is plain
that the practical involvement in military life of Gallus and
Tibullus, and the personal bitterness and consequent scepticism
about war that we discern in Propertius are equally remote
from Ovid. Though a knight, he had not served in the army
and his family seems not to have taken the wrong side in the
Civil War. He therefore deploys the now conventional themes
and motifs of the poet rejecting the glory and rewards of war
in favour of the battles of the bedroom, but he cannot bring
them to life, they are mere decoration. Coming at the end of
the brilliant line of Roman elegiac poets, he develops to their
ultimate conclusion, not the elegists' anti-war attitudes or their
contempt for military rewards and glory, but rather the anti-
Augustan moral and social standards implicit in their work.

Ovid fleshes out the picture of the elegist as presented in the
poetry that survives. He has turned away from the conventional
standards of service and success in Roman life; he rejects politics, military life, and financial gains. Whether his preference
is for the quiet life of the country or for starving in a garret in
Rome, he is dominated by only two driving forces, his mistress
(or boy friend) and the writing of a certain type of poetry. In

the first instance, he is rejecting also the restrictive but prag-
matic norms of sexual behaviour to which most Romans, including Augustus in his official capacity at any rate, paid lip service.
In the second instance, he is rejecting a dominant tradition of
Roman literature at the very period in which it was being
assiduously reinvigorated.

Let us examine the implicit morality of elegy first. Whether
the elegist attributes his misery (or amazing happiness) to madness or witchcraft, he claims to live a very private, if not a dis-
ordered and anti-social, life (in Propertius' words, *nullo vivere
consilio*, 1.1.6). Horace gives the sensible Roman's attitude to
such goings-on in the second satire of his first book, where he
criticizes those who go mad over freedwomen (presumably the
status of Cynthia, Delia, Nemesis, Corinna and the rest) and
who waste their money and ruin their good name. The elegist
will neither marry – this is the implication of Propertius' hatred
of chaste girls of good social standing (*castas odisse puellas*,
1.1.5)[1] – nor will he do what Horace does, enjoy the easily
available embraces of ordinary prostitutes. We noticed earlier
that Horace's few references to elegists are slightly contemptuous: he tells both Albius (Tibullus) and Valgius to stop their
unmanly complaints of lost loves, to desist from *flebiles modi* or
miserabiles elegi (*Od.* 2.9.9; 1.33.2 and *passim*). Valgius he
even invites to celebrate, as Horace does (despite his occasional
love poetry), the new battle honours of Augustus (*nova Augusti
tropaea*, *Od.* 2.9.18–19).

The professed aims and ideals of the elegists, however playfully they are interpreted, clearly and consciously fly in the
face of accepted Roman standards of seriousness, sobriety, public
service, and personal ambition. This is obvious from the defiant,
or half-apologetic, defences that they offer of their way of life.
The standard estimate of a poet's social utility and status is best
seen in Cicero's defence of Archias, although Archias was admittedly a foreigner by descent (cf. e.g. *Pro. Arch.* 9, 12). The
elegists, by and large, although they have abnegated their Roman
duty of 'praising famous men' (and cities), direct their aspirations to the sort of fame that few conventional Romans would
seriously desire: this, along with their mistresses' affections, is

---

1 For the interpretation, see chapter 3 below, pp. 102–4.

their compensation for any lack of money, military distinction, or political power.

Augustus, however, whatever the deficiencies of his own personal life (and they were many), had set himself seriously to the task of amending Roman public morals. He did not have to cope with drugs and he does not seem to have been worried about drink. He was, however, troubled by the decay of religion – Polybius, after all, had attributed Rome's greatness partly to her dependence on superstition as a means of controlling the populace (6.56). Augustus was disturbed by the decline in sexual morality, by the prevalence of bachelorhood, which he thought responsible for a declining birthrate, and by anti-social behaviour in general; and he was offended by the conspicuous consumption of the upper classes.

The elegists all were, or pretended to be, poor, and so they would scarcely be the target of Augustus' sumptuary laws, but their sexual habits, or at least the sexual attitudes implicit in their work, might well raise Augustan eyebrows. Propertius and Ovid were, in their different ways, the main offenders.

Propertius announces his distaste for respectable ladies (1.1.5); he rejects military service because of Cynthia's tears (1.6 etc.); he refuses to produce any public-spirited celebration of the regime's military achievements (2.1 etc.); and, in one of his most straightforward poems, he even criticizes Augustan marriage legislation.

In this particular poem (2.7), there is a strong basic criticism of the regime. Propertius informs us Cynthia was overjoyed because the law that might separate the two lovers had been withdrawn. This was, presumably, the proposed *lex de maritandis ordinibus* which would have forced Propertius, a bachelor, to marry. According to Suetonius (*Aug.* 34), this rather strict law could not get through because of the public protest of those involved – which may indicate that even Augustus had his troubles with dissenters. But Propertius goes on to say that even Jupiter cannot divide two lovers against their will. Caesar may be powerful, but only in war; military conquests count for nothing when it comes to love. Propertius would sooner be condemned to death than betray his beloved and marry. It is not for Propertius to produce arrow-fodder for future military ventures against Parthia. No son of mine, he says, will be a soldier. If Cynthia can love him, then this will be worth more than his duties to family tradition.

The point about this poem is not so much the objection to the proposed legislation, although that is significant enough, but, in the context, the almost gratuitous rejection of the Roman duty to produce sons for the Roman Empire.

This of course is mild by comparison with Ovid's explicit message in the *Ars Amatoria*, which was, after all, the *official* reason for his banishment, even if, as so often with political crimes, there were deeper causes, or other more political poems, to take into account.

The anti-Augustan implications of the *Ars Amatoria* may be construed differently. The work may be seen as a parody of Vergil's *Georgics*, but aimed at keeping men *in* the city. If the *Georgics* be taken as supporting Augustus' land policies, the *Ars Amatoria* may be taken as doing the opposite for Augustus' moral legislation. But without going so far, one can find in the work, not just the encouragement to anti-social immorality at which Augustus professed umbrage, but more specific and less guarded irreverence about the larger ideals of the principate. To take an obvious example: in Book 1 of the *Ars* (177ff.) Ovid launches into a great apostrophe of Augustus' future conquests. Caesar plans to add what is missing to the Roman empire; the East will finally be ours; the Parthians will pay the penalty for what they did to Crassus and his son and the lost standards:

> ecce, parat Caesar, domito quod defuit orbi,
>   addere: nunc, Oriens ultime, noster eris.
> Parthe, dabis poenas; Crassi gaudete sepulti
>   signaque barbaricas non bene passa manus.
>   (*A.A.* 1.177–80)

The elaboration of the eulogy is long: Ovid is to write thanksgiving poems about Gaius Caesar's victories and he will of course watch the great triumph. But suddenly we discover that all of this is prelude to advice on how to pick up a girl in the crowd watching the procession. The lover is to invent fictitious names and nationalities for sections of the spectacle if necessary; he is even to use the victory banquets as an occasion for sexual encounters. Ovid, of course, is using, and elaborating, the Propertian motif of the lover watching the triumph go by while he clings to his girl, but there can be no mistaking the similarly deflating effect of moving from the military sublime to the ridiculously sexual. The Roman reader would easily detect therefore an ironic scepticism in Ovid's enthusiasm and praise. Indeed, one may note in passing that Ovid almost quotes from Propertius' notorious poem on Actium (*gaude, Crasse, nigras si quid sapis inter harenas*, 4.6.83), which may give pause to those who take it too seriously. Rhetorical inflation followed by deflation is not a technique peculiar to Juvenal, and Propertius was the pioneer in this mode. In my opinion, all of this is implied in Propertius 3.4, and the comparison is further evidence that much of Ovid's amatory work is 'Propertius vulgarized'.

In the midst of his advice to the fair sex – for Ovid, within his limits, was one of the first advocates of Women's Liberation in some matters – Ovid throws out a perfunctory disclaimer that his didactic treatise is not to be taken as directed against upper- and middle-class marriage. He was, he says, about to go over the ways to deceive a sharp husband and his watchful guards, but really wives *should* fear their husbands; brides *should* be watched: this is proper and this is what the laws, the emperor and propriety command. He will therefore direct his advice to the seduction of freedwomen (although not a word need be changed to make it applicable to more exalted ladies):

> nupta virum timeat, rata sit custodia nuptae:
> hoc decet, hoc leges duxque pudorque iubent.
> > (A.A. 3.613–14)

The penalty for Ovid was harsh, whereas Propertius was luckier; the punishment did not perhaps fit the alleged crime; but the anti-Augustanism of the *Ars Amatoria* and the work of Propertius on which it was based need not be glossed over in our pity for Ovid and our understanding of Propertius' obliqueness.

Literature and politics

Such an analysis of the elegists' political and social attitudes is relatively uncomplicated. When we turn to the politics of literature, other more complex factors enter. Purely personal considerations of life-style, patronage, and past history will no longer suffice to explain why this poet or that writes in one particular vein. The evidence is treacherous, but it is possible to discern some tendencies and connections that will explain certain aspects of the literary divisions in the Augustan age.

The word *Augustan* has many connotations and it is best, for our purposes here, to use it simply as a chronological term. In the past, it has had a rather lulling effect on critics. In another context, that of English literature, A. R. Humphries has perceptively pointed to similar dangers in the word: when we dub the century in which *our* Augustan period fell 'The Age of Reason', we are creating 'the impression . . . that by some psychological freak three or four generations of Britons grew up colour-blind to the emotions'. He suggested 'that if the Augustans spoke so much of reason it was not because their emotions were weak but because on the contrary they were strong'.[2] Similarly, we sometimes forget, partly because of the associations of the word *Augustan* in English literary history, that Vergil, Horace and Propertius emerged not from some Arcadia or from the political background of Queen Anne, but from a hard, dangerous, troubled, and often bloody historical reality: as Tacitus puts it, 'after this there was undoubtedly peace, but it was a bloody peace' (*pacem sine dubio post haec, verum cruentam, Ann.* 1.10). Some of our sources may exaggerate the facts, but his part in the proscriptions, his behaviour after the siege of Perusia, and his ruthless elimination of serious opposition during his rise to power, surely merit for Augustus Syme's description of him as 'a chill and mature terrorist'.[3] In our own time, the Spanish Civil War offers copious analogies, although *los cuatro generales* did not last as long as the *triumviri*. (Franco himself, of course, survived even longer than Augustus.)

Classical literature often seems the imposition of form on a troubled reality, whether it be the turbulence of Periclean Athens

---

2 A.R. Humphries, *The Augustan World, Life and Letters in Eighteenth-Century England* (London 1964) 189.

3 R. Syme, *The Roman Revolution* (Oxford, 1939, 1960) 191.
Cf. also pp. 187ff., 202ff., 476ff., 490ff., where Tacitus' judgement is amply documented.

or the post-Civil War period in Rome. But because Vergil, Horace and Ovid are the standard Latin classics from this era, one must not be tempted into assuming that they personally invented and then unanimously accepted their new unimpeachable standards of art. One must bear in mind that Horace's three books of *Odes* met with a disappointing reception; that many still preferred the satires of Lucilius to Horace's gentler, if more artistic, brand of *sermones*; that Vergil for his *Aeneid* was described by Agrippa as the inventor of a new type of parody or bad imitation (*novae cacozeliae repertorem*), an attack that was followed up by numerous critics in the next generation – not least by the author of the *Aeneidomastix*, 'A Whip for the *Aeneid*'; that even Vergil's *Eclogues* were cruelly parodied by contemporary poets; that Tibullus, Valgius, and Propertius were given short shrift for their elegies by Horace. In brief, one must bear in mind the excited literary controversies of the period, the rivalries, the critical backbiting, the disagreements, often with political implications, out of which were slowly produced the very different kinds of masterpieces that have come down to us, whose differences, since they are now all classics, may be easily overlooked. We need to locate on a critical map the positions of the Augustan poets that will do justice to their divergent principles and the opposing traditions of literature that they embraced. The political implications of their choices might then also emerge. The controversies of the period are reminiscent of the literary-cum-political fights that were, and are, so prevalent in Soviet literature in the past fifty years, from Gorky to Solzhenitsyn.

A would-be poet of the Augustan era, about to enter the Battle of the Books, from which he might carry away fame, patronage, and financial rewards, had a number of literary and practical decisions to make. In prose writing, history, for example, he would have had to decide whether his sympathies lay with the Republican cause or the New Order, an alternative which a poet might be able to avoid by taking up a genre which did not involve such considerations. If he looked to his potential public, he would see a choice between the respectable, high-minded older Romans, with their preferences for archaic and Republican literature, and the younger, more permissive, and sophisticated audience at which Ovid's *Ars Amatoria* was so clearly directed.

More select audiences included the patrons of literature and their informal circles – Asinius Pollio, Messala, Maecenas, and, above all, the literate emperor himself. Augustus had his own critical principles – he hated archaism and Asianism, for example – and he was even something of a writer. But his literary outlook was also affected by concern for his public image, his political status, and his moral legislation. Only the best artists were allowed to treat of Augustus and his achievements, and both T. Labienus, the supporter of Pompey, and Ovid were, among others, the targets of indignant censorship.[4]

Apart from these extrinsic considerations, there were at least two major traditions, not always separable, from which to choose. In the last days of the Republic, the most notable poetic movement was the Neoterics, the circle or series of circles that looked to Alexandria, to Callimachus, Philitas, Euphorion, and Theocritus, for their inspiration: these included such writers as Catullus, Varro of Atax, Calvus, Gallus, and others. And it is plausibly argued that the emigré Parthenius of Nicaea was an important mediator and teacher of this *avant-garde* movement.[5] Its preference was for the newer, smaller poetic genres: epigram, elegy, the so-called 'epyllion', pastoral, didactic and, naturally, gently teasing court poetry. This tradition was characterized by metrical and formal experimentation, oblique and *recherché* treatment of myth, and, in general, an avoidance of epic, certainly on contemporary subjects or of ambitious scope, as exemplified by the Cyclic poets and Ennius' *Annales*.

Against this was the older tradition that descended from Ennius, to himself and later generations the Roman Homer. Its adherents admired the writings of Accius, Pacuvius, Lucilius and the antique style in general; they looked for public-spirited poetry on a grand Roman scale. Just as Catullus is contemptuous of the long *Annales* of Volusius (36, 95), so Cicero, a practitioner himself in this Roman tradition, sneers at the Neoterics, the *cantores Euphorionis* (*Tusc. Disp.* 3.45).

These basic traditions, of course, follow their own develop-

---

4 Note in particular Tac. *Ann.* 1.72: *primus Augustus cognitionem de famosis libellis specie legis eius tractavit . . .*
5 See W.V. Clausen, 'Callimachus and Roman poetry', *GRBS* 5 (1964) 193ff., and chapter 4 below.

ment as we enter the Augustan age. The metrics of each are refined and developed, an obvious example being the gradual
elimination in elegy of polysyllabic pentameter endings.[6] The
divisions between them blur. New modes, more difficult to characterize as belonging to one side or another, are developed; and
poets following their own artistic bent, borrow and blend from
each. The more slavish adherents to one tradition or another, the
hard core of minor poets, might have presented a clearer picture of the basic literary situation than individual and original
geniuses, but they have doubtless failed to survive simply because of this unoriginality. It is difficult to estimate how much
we have lost: how many panegyrical epics on contemporary wars,
such as the *Bellum Aquitanicum* of Cornelius Severus and how
many laborious Alexandrian mythological poems such as the
Zmyrna of Calvus and *The Grove of Grynium* of Cornelius
Gallus.[7]

But, despite this, two opposing tendencies in the undercurrent
of critical comment, or even parody, in the poetry that survives
from the period may be detected. Horace, for example, hews
largely to the Roman line for all his own innovations, but he is
critical of those who admire only archaic poets and archaic language, while ignoring those moderns who are producing a newer,
more stylish, embodiment of their virtues. His earlier work, the
Satires, descended directly from Ennius and Lucilius, but he
strenuously objected to those uncritical admirers of Lucilius who
did not see Horace's stylistic superiority. Horace's admiration for
Greek literature, for Homer, Old Comedy, etc., is of course obvious; he even borrows not a little from the Alexandrian and
neo-Alexandrian writers – Callimachus' and Philodemus' epigrams, for instance – when writing his lighter odes and the *Satires*. For his more substantial odes and epodes on political and
social themes, he preferred to go back to the great age of Greek
lyric – to Pindar, Bacchylides, Sappho, and Alcaeus. We have
already noticed his dislike or contempt for the most flourishing

6 Not necessarily a poetic gain: see B. Axelson, 'Der Mechanismus
   des ovidischen Pentameterschlusses', *Ovidiana*, ed. N.I. Herescu
   (Paris 1958) 121–35.
7 See, however, H. Bardon, *La Littérature latine inconnue* II
   (Paris 1956) 11ff.

Alexandrian genre at this time, love elegy, whereas he often praises or encourages writers, or potential writers, of epics that would celebrate the war-like achievements of Augustus and his generals.

Vergil, on the contrary, began as an Alexandrian writer, who did his best to reconcile the public themes that the Roman tradition advocated with the stylistic and thematic objectives of his models. Under pressure from his circle and circumstances, if the stories are true in the *Lives of Vergil*, he moved more and more in the direction Horace had taken early. His Theocritean imitations have more politics in them than his model; his *Georgics*, although a didactic poem and acceptable therefore by strict Alexandrian standards, share many of the purposes of Horace's protreptic odes and *Satires*; that is, they conform to the political and social ideas of the regime. This is not, of course, to condemn the work out of hand – not all good literature is the literature of protest. And finally, in the *Aeneid*, although there are many Alexandrian elements in his treatment, such as the Dido episode and the aetiological interest of the story of Hercules and Cacus, Vergil has finally taken his stand with the Roman tradition, producing an epic to the glory of Rome and its great past and present heroes. For all the many heart-searchings and pessimistic doubts about Rome's destiny, in Book 4 Vergil firmly makes Aeneas choose War, not Love.

On this spectrum of public versus private themes; of Rome versus Alexandria; of Love versus War; of epic versus elegy; of public law versus private disorder, the elegists are clearly to the left of Horace and Vergil.

Propertius' dilemma

Propertius' poetry shows the tension most clearly. He openly claims as his masters Philitas and Callimachus, whose Roman equivalent he hopes to be; he rejects war, conquest and money-making for the private pursuits of love, learning, and poetry. Yet he came into Maecenas' orbit for a short time; he is aware of the power of Augustus and the current Roman ideals of moral reform, the extension of empire, civilization, and the rule of law; he acknowledges the grander scale of epic by comparison with the softer, delicate nature of elegy (epic is *durus, grandis*; his verse is *tener, mollis*). For him all this constitutes pressure, internal or external, exaggerated or real. Yet he rejects the pressure, and the manner of his rejection is illuminating both for his poetry and the literary history of the time. His chief reasons, or excuses, are the ineluctable claims of his mistress and the contrary pulls of his own genius and poetic inspiration, generally personified as Apollo (3.3). His main shield is the *recusatio*, the formal poetic rejection of a given theme, which takes various forms, either the elaborate defence of his refusal to write epic or an account of his intention and aim to do so, which is then frustrated by divine warnings. It may even take the form of inviting Maecenas to do so first, or invoking Vergil's earlier Alexandrian work in his defence (cf. 3.9; 2.34.67ff.).

This tension is best seen in Books 2 and 3. Book 1 is more like Tibullus' work; the question had not arisen, for Propertius had not yet come into contact with Maecenas' circle. Had he done so, the fact would not have gone unrecorded. With Book 4, things change. The case generally made, as we observed earlier, is that Propertius, much like Vergil in a different, more extreme way, came to terms with the claims of the regime and the claims of his art. There was one Alexandrian sub-genre of elegy, aetiological elegy on origins, legends, and causes, which was both sanctioned by Callimachean principles and capable of being adapted to the service of Roman greatness. Hence the series of elegies on Roman or Italian deities and religious institutions; on the history of the *spolia opima*; on the story of Tarpeia. They are of course the main models for Ovid's *Fasti*, further confirmation of the view that Ovid's facility vulgarizes Propertius' more complex essays in elegiac genres. This final bowing to imperial pressures, it is suggested, is confirmed by the long and strange elegy on Octavian's victory at Actium which scholarly opinion characterizes as, to be charitable, somewhat below the level of Propertius' best work.[8] The rest of the elegies in this book, the

---

8 To be more accurate, G.W. Williams described it in *JRS* 52 (1962) 43, as 'one of the most ridiculous poems in the Latin language.' In *Tradition and Originality in Roman Poetry* (Oxford 1968) 51, the statement is somewhat toned down: 'Propertius is generally judged to have written a thoroughly bad poem.'

poems on Cynthia and related private or traditional themes, are either make-weight compositions, introduced for variety, or else the whole book is a non-unified posthumous compilation by an editor, who gathered together the few finished aetiological poems and interspersed with them poems that belonged to an earlier stage of Propertius' literary career.

At the risk of being repetitious, there is much to object to in this account. It involves a complicated explanation of the first long and clearly programmatic elegy, regardless of whether this is one poem or a diptych. In this poem Propertius announces his project of an account of Roman religion, festivals, and ancient topographical nomenclature, a project which is hardly justified, anyway, by the few extant aetiological elegies. The poet is then taken to task by the astrologer Horos and told to write love elegy as before:

> 'at tu finge elegos, fallax opus: haec tua castra
>   scribat ut exemplo cetera turba tuo.
> militiam Veneris blandis patiere sub armis,
>   et Veneris pueris utilis hostis eris.'   (4.1.135–8)

> *'But you must write elegy, a deceptive genre: this*
> *where your standards are planted and where all the*
> *other writers will follow your example. Soldier on in the*
> *campaigns of Venus – her weapons are sweet – and you*
> *will be a handy target for her Cupids.'*

Moreover, the private poems to Cynthia are far superior to the aetiological elegies with which they are inmixed. Even these elegies have certain ambiguous features, certain elements of humour and anti-Augustan touches which tell against the conventional interpretation.[9] A case may therefore be made that Book 4 is in fact Propertius' most subtly anti-Augustan production, in which he *proves* that he is not suited to even the most artistically congenial way of supporting the programme of the regime. The strange, *deliberately* or *unavoidably*, odd poem on Actium (4.6 at the very centre of the collection) is the final confirmation of his point. In a later chapter we may speculate whether Proper-

---

9 See my *Ezra Pound and Sextus Propertius*, 61ff.

tius genuinely tried to write worthwhile Roman aetiological elegies and then failed; or wrote so few because they went against his grain from the beginning: in either case, we may now understand the significance of the opening elegy and the importance for him of the other love poems which stand in the book as proof of his still impressive talent for love poetry. After this, death, caution, or failing inspiration enjoined his silence.

Ovid as Propertius' successor

The torch passes to Ovid. He, of course, was more than an elegist, but both in his early work and in his later *Metamorphoses* he made clear to which tradition he belonged, for all his facility and poetic versatility. And his eventual fate was to be determined, among other things, by his literary politics. It seems fairly clear, at least until the axe fell in A.D. 8 or so, that Ovid, unlike Propertius and perhaps Tibullus, did not feel the strain of the times; the Civil Wars ended when he was still a mere boy; the clear domination of the *princeps* was a fact of life that he could contrast with no other form of political existence. Deprived of avenues for real ambition, it was natural that the *jeunesse dorée* of Rome, Ovid's contemporaries and audience, would turn to less strenuous amusements and pursuits than the old *cursus honorum*. Had Ovid been born in a different time, his virtuosity in poetry might well have been directed to more public themes, to *littérature engagée*. But it would have been very strange for a talented author of a sophisticated, even sceptical, disposition to choose the Roman tradition over the Alexandrian tradition. There would have to be, of course, some conventional deference to the regime, a deference found in Alexandrian court poetry also, but the Alexandrian tradition, as now established in Rome by Catullus, Gallus, Propertius, Tibullus, and others, offered greater freedom of treatment and a wider range of subject-matter. Its themes did not have to follow a particular political line, simply because they were not, except subtly, incidentally, and occasionally, political. Consider however, what would happen to a poet – or any sort of writer for that matter – who chose the public domain for his material. Augustus' description of Livy as a Pompeian was jocular, but he was responsible for the fate of the lesser Pompeian, T. Labienus. In effect, the party line was, within limits, fixed; and dangers awaited those who went too far against it. It is not until a couple of generations had distanced the basic political controversy that a writer could feel freer, again within limits, to praise the losing side and give vent to Republican feelings: *victrix causa deis placuit, sed victa Catoni.* And it is hard to hold up Lucan as an example of free speech that went unpunished, for all his careful, or ironic, obeisance to the ruling Caesar.

Ovid in the period before his exile was arguably the most Alexandrian, although not the most poetically gifted, of all the elegists. There is little of the soul-searching that Propertius thought it proper to display; little of the inconsistency of Tibullus towards war. The Callimachean principles are perhaps too obviously and rhetorically embodied; but Propertian irony towards the current literary and political ideas, and towards the *princeps* was only too gladly (and perilously) imitated. Perhaps everything seemed well in the new, less warlike, less political, more affluent society of Rome after 20 B.C., when the great expansionist cries were heard less and less and a more rational frontier policy was developed.

Ovid, of course, worked elegy to death; unlike Roman satire, Roman love elegy died as a serious art form within half a century. But the young elegist still remained true to his Alexandrian principles, even when he abandoned elegy. In versifying the Roman calendar in elegiacs he had, of course, Propertius' example to draw upon, but Ovid progressed to more grandiose artistic endeavours. Elegists, of course, as their self-conscious apologies show, always admitted that there were greater forms of art: they were just dubious whether modern writers could achieve success in them. Ovid, however, did not embrace the Roman tradition that other elegists attacked or deferred to: namely, epic, whether historical, contemporary, or mythological, although it would be absurd to say that he did not have the talent for it. Instead, he chose an Alexandrian form, for whose authenticity he could invoke Callimachus' *Aetia* and Nicander's *Heteroeoumena.* He embarked on the *Metamorphoses,* a *carmen perpetuum,* which was not an *aeisma dienekes* in the bad sense Callimachus meant it, an epic,[10] but rather a cunningly interlocking series of 'epyllia', elegiac themes, panegyrics, aetiological investigations, didactic lessons, and the rest. It is in effect an Alexandrian counter-epic. And there by now, dominating the literary-political scene, was the target: Vergil's *Aeneid*. Unfortunately, Ovid, perhaps because of the times or his own self-confidence, was not as subtle and ironic in his attack on the official literary and political Establishment and he suffered the fate that Propertius had, by death or discretion, avoided.

10 See my review of Brooks Otis, *Ovid as Epic Poet* (Cambridge 1966) in *The Arch* 14.2 (1967) 1–9.

3
CYNTHIA PRIMA FUIT

The critical problems

In conventional regard, difficult to gainsay, Propertius' love affair
with Cynthia dominates the bulk of his poetry before Book 4.
The problem is to approach the material critically. In simpler
days it was assumed that the first three books faithfully recorded
the beginnings and the end, with all the joys and miseries in
between, of a long relationship between a younger poet and a
disreputable, talented, and cruel, older woman, even though
there were those who contrasted unfavourably the contrived and
Alexandrian complexities of Propertius' narrative to the directness of Catullus' love poetry.

Lachmann, Plessis and others even thought that they could
give us almost a blow by blow chronology of the affair. An
intense beginning when Propertius was 18; a year's painful rejection by her; then five years' uneasy devotion, between 29 and
24 B.C., which slowly cools into the final bitter rejection of 3.25,
after which Cynthia dies in poverty, but still dominates Propertius' imagination, reappearing to him as a ghost (4.7). But the
year of separation (*discidium*) is placed differently by different
scholars; five years is a conventional number; and a case might
be made for the relationship lasting ten years (29–19 B.C.).
There is even disagreement as to whether Cynthia was a *meretrix* or a married woman. What emerges from these discussions
is that elegiac poets are not historians nor are they on oath.

The reaction against the biographical approach to Roman
love poetry, like our own abandonment of romantic canons of
judgement, has been healthy: the lessons inculcated were well
taken and the gains should not be discounted.[1] Attempts to

---

1 Cf. e.g. H. Cherniss, 'Biographical fashion in literary criticism',
  U. of Cal. Publications in Class. Phil. 12 (1943) 279ff. and A.W.
  Allen, ' "Sincerity" and the Roman elegists', *CP* 45 (1950)
  145–60.

reconstruct the chronology of Propertius' liaison with Cynthia rested on a fundamental misunderstanding of the nature of poetry in general and love poetry in particular. But in guarding themselves carefully against this fallacy, more recent critics are retreating to critical vantage points of such moderate elevation that we are in danger of losing as much as we gain. The naive acceptance of a poem as a biographical document to be literally interpreted is being replaced by an obsession with form and structure and a greater dependence than ever on that stand-by of the classical critic, *Quellenforschung.*

Now the formal analysis of any work of art is all very well, but if it stops there it has no means of distinguishing between major and minor art, between the trivial and the significant, and it can, in extreme cases, result in some strange perversions of literary taste which base themselves on 'technical perfection'. At some point one has to reassert in some form or other the primacy, even in literature, of *life,* the parity of content with form and the parity of feeling with technique.

To take a simple example, poets frequently write on historical themes. A knowledge of poetic convention will allow us to discount comparisons of leaders with gods, exaggerated accounts of the events on the battlefield, or the water, but the invocation of poetic *personae* or artistically autonomous 'sincerity' cannot blur the fact that such and such an historical event took place and that the poet may be representing a general social reaction to that event. Were the poems of Propertius and Horace on the Battle of Actium the only evidence for that battle, would we be justified in denying its reality because of the poetic nature of the evidence? There are times and circumstances when it makes no sense for the poet to produce fiction instead of fact, however much the poetic licence he arrogates to himself. We must therefore distinguish in the light of our knowledge between those areas where poets are reliable witnesses because they have no motive for being otherwise and those areas where artistic conventions allow us to draw no inferences from the work itself.

'Who is Cynthia, what is shee . . . ?'

If this premise is allowed, then although we cannot determine dates in the affair or pinpoint the quarrels and the infidelities that occurred in the decline of the relationship, yet from both the internal and external evidence there emerges a fairly plausible portrait of Propertius' mistress. Whether in reality she had, to such a high degree, all the traits which Propertius attributes to her is a matter of small consequence. But assuming even a minimal relationship of literature to life and allowing for all the liberties and exigencies that poetic conventions impose, we may piece together a picture of Cynthia from our scanty literary evidence, our knowledge of the social and historical situation in Rome, and even Propertius' own words, where truth or poetic fiction would not be at issue.

Cynthia's real name, according to Apuleius (*Apol.* 10), was Hostia, which might imply a decent background. If we believe Propertius' reference to her literary grandfather (3.20.8 *docto avo*) and his praise of her own poetic and musical talents, this *docta puella* may have been the grand-daughter of Hostius, the author of an epic poem on the Istric War of 129 B.C., fought against the people inhabiting the peninsula above the modern Jugoslav town of Pula.[2] This is not very likely and it is, perhaps, better to assume that Propertius is simply flattering his mistress and associating her on the basis of her name with the poet.

Another, even less plausible, suggestion is that her name was Roscia and that Apuleius' text is corrupt.[3] This would link her to the comedian Q. Roscius Gallus, who was called *doctus* by Horace (*Ep.* 2.1.82) and whose family was connected with Lanuvium and the temple of Juno Caprotina there.[4]

What is clear from Apuleius' remarks is that the elegists and the other love poets were wont to give meaningful, and usually metrically equivalent, pseudonyms to their ladies. So Catullus' Clodia became 'Lesbia', in honour of Sappho, the poet's lyric model. Tibullus chose 'Delia' to pun on his *inamorata's* name, Plania, but the name had also connotations deriving from Apollo, the god of poetry and music. Ovid's 'Corinna', an imaginative

---

2 See R. Helm, *RE* 27 (1957) 761.
3 Proposed by A. Marx, *De Sexti Propertii vita et librorum ordine temporibusque* (diss. Leipzig 1884) 47.
4 See further J.-P. Boucher, *Études sur Properce* (Paris 1965) 460–8.

composite if there ever was one,[5] incorporates a tribute to the
Boeotian poetess of that name. 'Perilla' was the literary name of
Ticidas' girl friend Metella, herself a poet (Apul. *Mag.* 10; Ov.
Trist. 3.7.1,29; 2.437), just as 'Cytheris' was the more euphonious
nom de guerre of Antony's mistress, Volumnia, whose stage
name was Lycoris.[6] Nor were such pseudonyms limited to
women. Even Lygdamus, the post-Augustan poet[7] of the Tib-
ullan corpus, may have chosen his *nom de plume* to incorporate
a Greek allusion to Albius, Tibullus' gentile name. The Romans
were not meticulous in their etymological puns and Bentley's
'Law' of the metrical interchangeability of name and pseudonym
describes only a tendency. Indeed, in the Tibullan corpus,
Sulpicia's Cerinthus may well be a pseudonym for Cornutus,
Tibullus' friend and a member of the so-called Messalan circle.
Propertius, like many of his fellow love poets, presumably chose
Hostia's (or Roscia's) pseudonym out of deference to Apollo,
whose cult name Cynthius derives from his birth on Delos,
where Mt Cynthus stands. Indeed, because his sister Artemis,
identified with Diana by the Romans, was also born there and
so could be referred to as 'Cynthia' (Hor. *Od.* 3.28.12; Ov. *Met.*
2.465; *et al.*), and since Diana was also Luna, the goddess of
the moon (Sen. *Herc. Oet.* 641; Luc. *Phars.* 1.218), the choice
of the name was perhaps, in current parlance, 'over-determined',
although it does not, to my mind, justify the ingenious speculation about the connection, in Propertius' mind and poetry, between his mistress and that celestial body. His friend, Tuscus,
is perhaps addressed in his second book as 'Demophoon', because his lady-love had been given the pseudonym 'Phyllis' and
Theseus' son, Demophoon, had loved the Thracian princess of
that name (cf. Ov. *Pont.* 4.16.20). For similar linguistically
allusive reasons, Lynceus (2.34) has been identified as the
famous L. Varius Rufus, friend of Vergil and Horace.
  Cynthia's real name, then, was probably Hostia and Proper-

5 See my 'Two problems in Roman love elegy', *TAPA* 92 (1961)
  522-8; *contra* P. Green, 'Venus Clerke Ovyde' in *Essays in
  Antiquity* (London 1960) 109-35.
6 See *RE* 4 (1345) *s.v. 'Cornelius'*.
7 See A.G. Lee, 'The date of Lygdamus and his relation to Ovidius',
  PCPhS 5 (1958/9) 15-22.

tius' flattering comments about her background were intended
to take advantage of this fact. But what of her appearance
and character?

Over-valuation of a love object is to be expected in both
lovers and poets. Nevertheless, it is unlikely that a poet will
describe a blonde mistress as a brunette, even if, like Propertius,
he is ready enough to compare her to goddesses and heroines.
We may therefore take Propertius' description of his mistress'
appearance and character with no more than a grain of salt.
Cynthia's eyes and beauty attracted him first as elegy 1 of Book
1 makes clear. She had a milk-and-roses complexion. Her long
blonde hair was either over-elaborately groomed or else, in less
guarded moments, it strayed over her forehead in disarray
(2.1.7). Those attractive eyes were black. She was tall, with
long slim fingers, and it would seem that she was extravagantly
fond, to Propertius' dismay, of cosmetics and elegant clothes.
Propertius' distress seems largely due to his suspicion of her
motives in adopting her extravagant style of adornment. More
charitably one might suppose that the real reason for her interest in such extraneous aids was her advancing years.[8]

Propertius, however, does not defend his violent passion
simply because of Cynthia's striking physical characteristics. He
constantly stresses her sensuality, her interest in the arts, both
domestic and cultural, and her passionate, if violent, disposition.
He realizes that the fury of their relationship is part of Cynthia's
attraction for him. Her unpredictability, her lies, and her infidelities, are part of this disposition and he seems, at times, to be
aware of the part these traits play in the relationship. He frequently professes forgiveness for her wayward ways and curses
those lovers who have a peaceful relationship with their mistresses:

> a pereat, si quis lentus amare potest.   (1.6.12)

Not for Propertius the joys of a tranquil relationship. For the

---

8 For further details and the references, see Saara Lilja, *The Roman
Elegists' Attitude to Women* (Helsinki 1965) 122–6. One may note
that, because of its rarity in Italy, blonde hair at this period was
particularly fashionable. Imported blonde hair was in
frequent use, particularly among disreputable women, and we
discover from 2.18 that Cynthia's blondness came out of a bottle.

causes of this, as we shall see later, Propertius' psychohistory must be investigated.

Roman love poetry

I alluded earlier to the necessity of asserting the primacy of *life,* in its broadest sense, in our judgements of literature. We cannot, I believe, restrict ourselves, as is the current fashion, to not-so-New Criticism and to the explication of individual poems as though they existed in a literary and social vacuum.

Latin elegy, where we must include Catullus since Propertius regards him as a forerunner, is a key case. We might imagine it, simplistically, as the product of a sentiment parallel to modern sentiment; we might see it as artificial and unsympathetic because of the poetic conventions and mythological themes it utilizes, forgetting how highly artificial in certain ways are some of our own paradigms of love poetry, such as Donne's elegies and Shakespeare's sonnets; we might dismiss it, as does C. S. Lewis,[9] as the product of exhibitionism, the product of what are taken to be simply the traditional classical attitudes to sex, the frankly sensual or the timorously distrustful, according to which love is simple physical pleasure or plain madness, and the Palace of Love a brothel or a bedlam.

But good poets are more than the skilful manipulators of forms and literary traditions and do more than represent with documentary fidelity the standard attitudes of the culture from which they emerge. The best poets are usually the growing points of a culture and at least bear witness to its sensibility at its most developed, even when they are not themselves moulding it. For any age except our own (where we have privileged access), how society thinks and feels on the most important human topics can be most clearly judged from its literature; yet it is in its literature too that we must look for the finest and most sensitive (and the most unorthodox) developments of an age's attitudes. We may also, it is true, find in its literary works apparently representative norms, which, when backed by factual evidence such as the Pompeian *bordelli,* are easily taken to be

9 *The Allegory of Love* (Oxford 1936) 5.

the sexual *mores* of a society. But because literature does more than represent standard attitudes, such literary evidence has to be handled very carefully. Would we judge, on the one hand, Victorian sexual morality by the novels of Dickens or, on the other hand, twentieth-century *mores* by Nabokov's *Lolita* or Henry Miller's *Tropic of Capricorn?*

The Roman elegists have suffered from assimilation, both to each other and to very different writers like Horace and Juvenal, and this had led to a false picture of their work and the society from which it emerged. Classical attitudes to sex and love *did* differ considerably from our own – marriage and homosexuality are obvious areas of difference. And it would be true to say that two main attitudes to heterosexual love can be distinguished: the conception of love simply as a physical appetite on a par with the appetites for food and drink, and the conception of love as a dreaded madness – whose object is undifferentiated, now a blood relative, now a social inferior, now a person of the same sex, now a member of a different species. Phaedra, Pasiphae, and Tereus are familiar mythological examples. Horace's *parabilis Venus facilisque*, sex with the prostitute and the slave, a mode of loving which Propertius' once contrasted favourably with his own in 2.23, and which was completely acceptable to models of Roman rectitude like Cato the Elder, represents the sensibility generally accredited to ancient civilization. Romantic homosexual alliances, examples of marital fidelity, self-sacrifice, and mutual love are not allowed to interfere with this general picture. But the truth is that the period covered by classical Greek and Roman literature, roughly a period of a thousand years, saw revolutions of sentiment comparable to certain revolutions in the modern period. A case could be made for Lesbian poetry, for the Greek novel, for Alexandrian epigram as indications of such revolutions, but at least one revolution, very adequately documented, took place in the last decades of Republican life.

The new women

Sentiment is dependent on social conditions, and cavemen no doubt lacked certain feelings we regard as basic. The first century B.C. in Rome witnessed the emergence of a new type of emancipated woman. In the Roman upper class there had always been women of strong character and influence, despite the theoretical supremacy of the *paterfamilias*. Legend had its Camillas and Lucretias, and history recorded its Gracchan Cornelias. But in the last century of the Republic and beyond, it is evident, there were women of strong character who did not follow the traditional pattern of dutiful daughter and patriotic wife. There were as well women of considerable personal power (exercised socially and politically), whose private lives departed considerably from traditional standards of feminine behaviour. Among such women may be mentioned the sisters of the wicked Clodius (one of whom is perhaps to be identified with Catullus' Lesbia) and Servilia, mistress of Caesar and mother of Brutus, a woman who exercised no little political influence. The phenomenon may be accounted for, along with so much else in late Republican Rome, by the freedom and moral laxity, the degeneration of the *prisca virtus*, so deplored by writers of the time as the consequence of the Punic wars. The explanations are matter for the social historian. But what is clear from the literary evidence is the high degree of social mobility at this period. The social turmoil of civil wars had for some its compensations. One result was certainly the growth of a recognizable *demi-monde*, which permeated upper- and middle-class society. Ex-slaves, lower-class free (or freed) women, actresses like Volumnia, the mistress of Gallus and Antony, even women of some family and independent means, but all women of some talent, comprised this group. They did not wear out their shoes along the Via Sacra or lurk in the tiny dens of the Subura. Their talents admitted them into the society of better-placed Romans, whether for *concubinatus* or more casual liaisons. Given such women, of high and low degree, naturally the classical views on the inferiority of woman became a little harder to uphold, and a Cleopatra did nothing to redress the balance. Women became persons rather than things, with characters of their own, not aggregations of ancient virtues.[10]

10 For a feminist interpretation of Propertius' attitude to Cynthia, see Judith P. Hallett, 'The role of women in Roman elegy: counter-cultural feminism', *Arethusa* 6 (1973) 103–20.

Catullus and Lesbia

A social revolution, of course, in no way necessitates a revolution of sentiment, but it is arguable that a certain sentimental revolution did take place. The first witness is Catullus and the poetry that emerges from his affair with Lesbia. The genius necessary for transmuting passion and experience into (good) art must not be underrated, but that some kind of revolution of sensibility has taken place seems undeniable, unless we approach his poetry with an eye prejudiced by the study of literary influences or by the belief in one simple classical attitude to love. In Catullus we have an analysis of an overpowering love, which is at first gladly accepted and gloried in:

> fulsere quondam candidi tibi soles,
> cum ventitabas, quo puella ducebat
> amata nobis, quantum amabitur nulla.   (8.3–5)

> *Once bright suns shone on you, when you used to go where the girl took you, loved by you as no other girl will be loved.*

Then we have the dialectic of disillusion, disillusion with someone who is not only heedless of him, but unworthy of his love:

> nullum amans vere, sed identidem omnium
>   ilia rumpens;
> nec meum respectet, ut ante, amorem,
> qui illius culpa cecidit . . .   (11.19–22)

> *loving no one truly, but time after time breaking all of their groins. Let her not think of my love as before; it is dead, thanks to her . . .*

This dialectic is as much occupied with the qualities and behaviour of Lesbia as it is with the subjective feelings of Catullus:

> nunc te cognovi: quare etsi impensius uror,
>   multo mi tamen es vilior et levior.   (72.5–6)

> *Now I know you. And so, although I am more extravagantly on fire for you, yet you are much cheaper and less faithful in my eyes.*

It cannot be assimilated to the usual classical analysis of passionate love as a simple madness, even though – and the cliché survives in more modern love poetry – Catullus, once disappointed, can pray to be delivered of it:

> o di, si vestrum est misereri, aut si quibus umquam
>> extremam iam ipsa in morte tulistis opem,
> me miserum aspicite et, si vitam puriter egi,
>> eripite hanc pestem perniciemque mihi . . .
>> (76.17–20)

> *O gods, if you have any pity, or if you have ever brought help to those at death's door, look down on me in my misery, and if I have led a pure life, take from me this destructive plague . . .*

But Catullus realizes that his problem is psychological, not theological:

> Huc est mens deducta tua, mea Lesbia, culpa
>> atque ita se officio perdidit ipsa suo,
> ut iam nec bene velle queat tibi, si optima fias,
>> nec desistere amare, omnia si facias. (75)

> *To this pitch has my heart been brought through you, Lesbia, and it has destroyed itself through its own steadfastness: it can no longer wish you well, though you became the best woman in the world, nor stop loving you, though you acted like the worst.*

Our love language too reflects the primitive belief in love as something sent from outside, something akin to madness, yet with us, and the same is arguably true of Catullus, it is accepted as part of the personality, as something worth defending and worth accepting. Lesbia is important not as a sexual object, but as a person:

> illa Lesbia, quam Catullus unam
> plus quam se atque suos amavit omnes . . . (58.2–3)

> *the Lesbia that Catullus loved alone and more than himself and his family . . .*

and it is not with the passion but with this person that Catullus is eventually at variance. The evidence is there in poems 5, 7, 8, 11, 43, 51, 58, 72, 76, 85, 92, 107 and 109. This is no love independent of the changes in its object nor is it a sensuality which can be purged or slaked:

> Nulla potest mulier tantum se dicere amatam
>> vere, quantum a me Lesbia amata mea est.
> nulla fides ullo fuit umquam foedere tanta,
>> quanta in amore tuo ex parte reperta mea est. (87)

> *No woman can say she has been loved as much, truly, as Lesbia has been loved by me. Never was there such fidelity in any union as was found on my side in loving you.*

Lesbia is important as an object of tenderness, of affection:

> dilexi tum te non tantum ut vulgus amicam,
>> sed pater ut gnatos diligit et generos. (72.3–4)

> *I loved you then not just the way anyone loves a mistress, but as a father loves his sons and sons-in-law.*

She is the object of a *romantic* love which can contemplate a permanent alliance:

> ut liceat nobis tota perducere vita
>> aeternum hoc sanctae foedus amicitiae. (109.5–6)

> *that we may be able for the whole of our lives to live eternally in this bond of holy affection.*

The trouble lies not in the utter absurdity of the passion (which should be the classical attitude), but in the misdeeds and callousness of the object of the passion (see 11.19–22 above).

Romantic love

It is unfortunate for the literary historian that we do not have the works of Varro, Calvus and Gallus, who were also Propertius' predecessors as love poets. Yet it is patent that Catullus had a good deal of effect upon Roman love elegy in general and Propertius in particular; he is clearly the pioneer. The lover represented in Propertius' poetry is, in subtle ways, different from the lover we descry in the Catullan poems, but both belong to the category of romantic lover; both fly in the face of classical attitudes to love. The tenderness of Catullus, the admiration and complaisance of Propertius, are typical of the romantic over-estimation of the love object. Their mistresses are their equals, if not, as Propertius pretends, their superiors. They are valuable not simply as beauties, but as possible friends and intellectual companions.

We are dealing with a revolution of feeling comparable to the sudden appearance in the Languedoc, at the end of the eleventh century, of Courtly Love, as represented in Troubadour poetry. And the comparison is instructive because Courtly Love has been partly explained as 'Ovid misunderstood'.[11]

The characteristics of Courtly Love have been described as Humility, Courtesy, Adultery, and the Religion of Love, and it has been called the 'feudalization of love'. Its object is another man's wife; its despairs spring from the obduracy of the lady or the possibility of a rival. Only men of culture could feel such love, and it necessitated a wilful flouting of the attitudes towards sex recommended by medieval Christianity. Some vestiges of this older attitude remain with us, but Courtly Love in general has been taken over and tamed by religious and social requirements – marriage is now conventionally, although less so in literature, the crown of our attenuated Courtly Love. This has social consequences best seen in America and parts of western Europe where the decay of romantic love inside a marriage or a new romantic attachment becomes a reason for divorce.

If 'Ovid misunderstood' is a way of looking at Courtly Love, it is also arguable that, for the modern reader, the earlier concentration on Ovid as a representative of elegiac love poetry has perhaps obscured the revolution of sensibility which may be seen in Catullus and Propertius. There is a real distinction between Ovid and the other practitioners of elegy. Ovid has been described as the generalizer of Roman love elegy; he is the 'general lover' and his Corinna has been usually regarded as a composite figure. But, of course, the 'general

11 See Lewis (n. 9 above), 7ff.

lover' is the seducer; one who adopts, for his own purposes, all the postures of the genuinely enamoured romantic lover. Ovid was an artist who followed in the steps of the *poetae novi*, such as Catullus, and their heirs, such as Propertius. It was not unnatural that he should also adopt one of their most important themes – Love. But the gulf between the love poetry of Catullus and Propertius and the love poetry of Ovid is immense. For Ovid seems to revert to 'classical' attitudes to women: Ovid, despite some liberated views about sex, degrades women, as the first book of the *Ars Amatoria* makes clear. They are not to be idealized: at best they are human, and at worst there is Pasiphae, the uncontrolled bestialist. Ovid offers her as a paradigm case to prove that women are easy prey for the predatory male. It is not mere chance that after Ovid Roman elegy was finished as a literary form. The amorous sensibility of the elegists was replaced by the sexual, if more human, cynicism of Ovid, which is present also in satirists like Petronius and Juvenal; and Ovid's over-facile versification made it impossible to return to the manner of the older elegists. Ovid was ready not only with advice on how to achieve 'the right true end of love,' but also with advice on the *Remedia Amoris*, the ways of extirpating a passion that was unproductive of happiness. This is not the frame of mind of the poet who said:

> mi neque amare aliam neque ab hac discedere fas est:
> Cynthia prima fuit, Cynthia finis erit. (1.12.19–20)

> *I have no right to love another or leave her: Cynthia was the first, Cynthia will be the end.*

If the formula 'Ovid misunderstood' is useful for an understanding of Courtly Love, then a correct view of that humorous, ironic parody of didactic poetry and love elegy will help us towards an understanding of earlier Roman love elegy. But it will be by way of contrast. In fact, when the troubadours 'misunderstood' Ovid they were returning to the sentiments and attitudes of the earlier Roman love poets. The similarities between Courtly Love and Propertius' attitude to love are closer to each other than either is to the traditional classical attitudes which Ovid so persuasively represents *(arte regendus amor)*.

Roman *gravitas*, in one case, and Christianity, in the other, put Propertius and the troubadour on the defensive; each worked through highly formalized poetic conventions. Beneath these conventions a similar sensibility may be discerned in both literatures, and both pose the same pseudo-problem of 'sincerity'. The 'feudalization of love', the humility of the lover, exemplified in the poets of the Languedoc, is paralleled by the *servitium amoris* of the Roman elegist; serf or slave, the human situation is roughly the same. Even the adulterous nature of Courtly Love may be paralleled in the elegist; the *vir,* the husband or the established lover, moves, a vague and thwarted figure, through the elegies of Tibullus and Ovid and the poetry of Catullus. Jealousy of course needs no dwelling upon, and the religion of love that we see in Troubadour poetry is paralleled by the frequent invocations and descriptions of Venus and Amor in Roman elegy (Tib. 1.6, Prop. 2.12, Ov. *Am.* 3.15) and the special religious status enjoyed by a lover (Prop. 3.16.11ff.), nor should it be overlooked that even the most sceptical Roman thinkers, such as Lucretius, were fully aware of what was symbolized by Venus and Cupid.

There are, of course, differences between the two sensibilities. There is little trace of some aspects of 'courtoisie' in the Roman elegists: blows and scratches are regarded as the common coin of reciprocated love and repeated reproaches part of it; there is less obvious *social* snobbery about who could and could not be a lover. But this should not hide the similarities between the love that we see in the Roman elegists, and Courtly Love, and therefore between the elegists' love and our own Romantic love. What to the truly classical author is an undesired madness becomes in the elegists a way of life, which they are prepared to defend against the claims and strictures of the more prudish older generation, against the claims of imperialist patrons, and indeed against the nagging doubts of their own Roman consciences. In an age in which individualism is automatically accepted as the right and obvious thing, it is easy to forget the tremendous strains imposed on the individual in a politically oriented society. Propertius seems to work hard to defend his poetic claims against various demands that he should write more national poetry, that he should choose more patriotic and imperial themes. But Propertius regarded his love poetry as inspired, and inspired by Cynthia *(ingenium nobis ipsa puella facit);* it was not a catharsis of an unworthy passion. It was defensible by the new canons of erotic poetry and the new standards of personal feeling.

The sensibility of Propertius is then much nearer that of our own age and the age of Courtly Love than it is to what are accepted as classical attitudes. We must be wary of approaching Roman love elegy backwards through Ovid, in whose work the counter-revolution had been already effected. It is not without significance that the appeal of Catullus and Propertius has steadily grown by contrast with the appeal of Ovid, despite his enormous popularity in the Middle Ages, the Renaissance and even later. Ovid had to be misunderstood by the troubadours to be adopted as their master; the psychological novel has made our perceptions too clear for us to be taken in by him as a real romantic. Ovid is anti-romantic, the cynical, worldly-wise seducer, who loves women, not a particular woman. Compared to Iseult, or indeed to Lesbia or Cynthia, Corinna is unreal. Even if we assumed that all the elegists in real life shared the same attitude to women, their literary creations would remain radically different. Such a difference can only be claimed as a difference of literary sensibility. Ovid may have been a tender husband, but as a poet of love he is, in a way he did not mean, merely a *tenerorum lusor amorum.*

'Romantic' is a confused term: if opposed to the classical conception of love, then Propertius, like Catullus, qualifies for it; if opposed to commonsense views, then all the Roman love poets in their work, except Ovid, qualify for it. They are all, except the sensible Ovid, as miserable as their poetry and perhaps their dispositions dictated. The term of course covers many things – an elopement, an adulterous liaison, even an unrealistic view of a future legal partner, may all be characterized as 'romantic'. The common element is that passion overmasters judgement, destroys the usual patterns of behaviour, and is impervious to friendly advice, social pressure, religious injunctions and personal standards. Such passion may be seen in most of the Roman elegists, just as it is found in more modern works of fiction as a socially acceptable motive which provides an alternative to the purely practical choice of a partner. Here, admittedly, it is domesticated and manages to compromise with older views of the emotion as anti-social and dangerous. There exists however in literature, as well as in life, a more disreputable form of romantic love which serves as an even better analogy for the splendours and miseries of the elegists, and which allows us to penetrate more deeply into the sensibility expressed in Propertius' poetry.

The pathology of passion

In a paper written in 1910,[12] Freud described a special type of love object chosen by some lovers and enumerated the conditions of love necessary for such men. These lovers are frequent characters in poetry and fiction and the classic example is the Chevalier des Grieux in Prévost's *Manon Lescaut*. The same type of lover may be seen in Dumas fils' *La Dame aux Camélias*, Proust's *Du Côté de chez Swann*, Dostoevski's *The Eternal Husband*, Somerset Maugham's *Of Human Bondage*, John O'Hara's *Butterfield 8*, and William Styron's *Lie Down in Darkness*. Freud's discussion, however, which is based on clinical observation, is clearer and more specific, for writers naturally have before them other aims than purely objective description. Nevertheless a familiarity with literary exemplars of this type of man will perhaps reconcile the reader to the use of Freud's *schema* for the investigation of a literary problem: How does Propertius characterize his relationship with Cynthia?

The conditions necessary for this type of man to fall in love are, according to Freud, as follows:

1 There must be an injured third party, whether a husband or a fiancé or an already established lover who has right of possession.

2 The woman must be one who is more or less sexually discredited, whose fidelity and loyalty admit of some doubt. She may be anything from a married woman to whom some breath

---

12 S. Freud, 'A special type of choice of object made by men', in *Collected Papers* IV (London 1953) 192–202.

of scandal attaches to a *grande amoureuse* or even a prostitute. Hence Freud's characterization of the passion as *Dirnenliebe*, the love of a harlot.

3 In normal love and in social convention a woman's value is measured by her sexual integrity. But this type of lover shows a striking departure from the norm, for they set the highest value upon the women they love. They do not use them and despise them, but regard them as the only women whom it is possible to love. Their relationships with them often absorb the whole of their mental energy to the exclusion of everything else.

4 These lovers set up an ideal of their own fidelity to the beloved, however often it may be shattered in reality.

5 Feelings of jealousy are a necessity for such men. Not until they have an occasion for jealousy does their passion reach its height and they never fail to seize upon some incident whereby this intensity of feeling may be called out. Most often this jealousy is directed against new acquaintances or strangers whom they suspect.

6 Most astonishing of all to the observer is a desire to 'rescue' the beloved. Such men are convinced that their beloved has need of them, that without them she would lose all hold on respectability and rapidly sink into degradation. They are saving her from this by not letting her go. And this trait is no less plain even when there is no real occasion for it. Freud instances a man who in such relationships devoted endless pains to composing tracts to keep his beloved on the path of 'virtue', that is, fidelity to himself.

Naturally the relative strength and prominence of these traits may vary in a given real (or fictional) case. Freud offers aetiological explanations of the genesis of this character-type. A high regard for the maternal image makes it impossible to fuse affection, respect, and sensuality. Passion is therefore only possible with a woman who is the unmistakable opposite of that maternal image.

Whatever the deeper psychoanalytical ramifications, we are, obviously, dealing with a recognizable class of men, common in both literature and life. And this purely descriptive summary

is all that needs be accepted in order to proceed with the in-
vestigation. For the character of the lover that emerges from
Propertius' poetry fits exactly the character-type described by
Freud, as is seen when the characteristics of the lover in Pro-
pertius are compared with the general traits enumerated by
Freud.

1 Although most of the poems probably deal with the period
when Propertius is already deeply involved with Cynthia, it is
plain that at some point, presumably early on in the relationship, the deception of another was necessary. Cynthia's ghost
recalls their early meetings:

> 'iamne tibi exciderant vigilacis furta Suburae
>   et mea nocturnis trita fenestra dolis?' (4.7.15–16)

> *'Had you forgotten already our stolen meetings in the
> watchful Subura and my window-sill worn by our noc-
> turnal deceptions?'*

Elsewhere he speaks of the door furtively opened to let him in
(2.9.42). Elegy 2.23 is an important document. Love entails
slavery (*nullus liber erit, si quis amare volet,* line 24), and this
slavery is compounded of dependence on another's whims and
the necessity of waiting until the lover or husband of one's
mistress is absent before one can see her:

> ingenuus quisquam alterius dat munera servo,
>   ut promissa suae verba ferat dominae? (3–4)

> *What free man gives presents to another man's slave, so
> that he will take his promised message to his mistress?*

The lover will hear his mistress say:

> '... Timeo, propera iam surgere, quaeso:
>   infelix, hodie vir mihi rure venit.' (19–20)

> *'I'm afraid, hurry and get up now, please; hard luck,
> today my man is coming back from the country.'*

Yet despite his protests against the clandestine nature of his
living and loving (*nolim furta pudica tori,* line 22) and his
occasional wistfulness for a girl who is openly for sale (*cui*

saepe immundo Sacra conteritur Via socco, line 15) or for the freer atmosphere of ancient Sparta (3.14.23–4), cuckolding is one of the didactic themes imposed upon him by Apollo:

> 'ut per te clausas sciat excantare puellas,
>   qui volet austeros arte ferire viros.'   (3.3.49–50)

> *'so that he who will wish to strike an artful blow at re-spectable husbands may know, through you, how to charm out cloistered young ladies.'*

and the subject of rivals replacing established lovers is not infrequent:

> Iste quod est ego saepe fui: sed fors et in hora
>   hoc ipso eiecto carior alter erit.   (2.9.1–2)[13]

> *What he is I often was: but, come chance and in an hour, another will be dearer than he, now cast out himself.*

> vinceris aut vincis: haec in amore rota est.   (2.8.8)

> *you are conquered or you conquer: this is the wheel of love.*

2 It should be plain from Cynthia's character as depicted by Propertius that his feelings for her must be regarded as a form of *Dirnenliebe.* But it should be emphasized that this form of *Dirnenliebe* is to be distinguished from the grosser forms it can take, where harlots are regarded at their proper worth and simply used for sexual gratification and where there is no question of any over-estimation of the beloved that love or passion entails. This use of the *parabilis Venus facilisque,* as Horace describes it (*Sat.* 1.2.119), was one of the ways of avoiding the *furor* of real love and one of the traditional *remedia amoris.*[14] No doubt Propertius knew of contemporaries who thus avoided his torments and he expressed his envy of them (2.23.13–14ff.), but this was not his real sexual orientation.[15] His was the pas-

13 Cf. also 1.8; 1.15; 2.8; 2.16; 2.34; 3.8.37ff.
14 See A.W. Allen, 'Elegy and the classical attitude toward love, Prop. I.1', YCS 2 (1950) 295–64.
15 This other sort of lover is described by Freud in a later paper, 'The most prevalent form of degradation in erotic life', *Collected Papers* IV (1953) 203–16.

sionate and romantic *Dirnenliebe*. And in no sense could Cynthia be regarded as a respectable woman, whatever her virtues. During the time of her affair with Propertius at least three rivals are specifically recorded as enjoying her favours, not to mention the frequent references to possible infidelities on her part (e.g. 1.8; 2.16; 3.8; 2.5.1ff.; 2.34.11). She was hardly a *grande amoureuse* like Catullus' Lesbia; she did not have the social standing for that. Indeed there are frequent references to her avarice, such as:

> Praetor ab Illyricis venit modo, Cynthia, terris,
>   maxima praeda tibi, maxima cura mei. (2.16.1–2)

> *A praetor has just come from Illyria, Cynthia, a great prize for you, a great worry for me.*

This poem and other references (e.g. 1.8.38; 2.8.11; 2.23.8; 2.24.11–16) indicate that in some ways she was almost a harlot. But in any event Propertius had no illusions about her character. She is *perfida* (2.5.3) and he says

> aut tecum aut pro te mihi cum rivalibus arma
>   semper erunt: in te pax mihi nulla placet. (3.8.33–4)

> *With you or for you against rivals, it will always be war for me: where you are concerned, there are no joys of peace for me.*

Yet he accepts her for what she is.[16] And this is not because he has no conception of fidelity or chastity (an ancient as well as a modern ideal) or that he does not value it in the conventional way. Not only does he cite mythological examples of fidelity, such as Penelope, Evadne and Hypsipyle (cf. 1.15.9ff.), when encouraging Cynthia to be faithful, but he also describes in glowing terms the fidelity of Aelia Galla (3.12).

3 Despite his portrayal of Cynthia as *dura* and *perfida*, there is no question of Propertius despising her for her lack of sexual integrity. Quite the contrary: however tormenting and painful be-

---

16 For the character and status of Cynthia, see also J. Fontenrose, 'Propertius and the Roman Career', *U. of Cal. Publications in Class. Philol.* 13 (1949) 373–6.

cause of her faults, his passion is for no unworthy object. Cynthia deserves his love, but unfortunately she does not behave as he thinks he would like her to behave, hence his sufferings, his complaints and his envy of those who are not in the grip of this *furor* (2.23). Once he is cured of his passion, he can then take a more objective view of her and realize he once over-valued her (3.24), but while in love with her he can at intervals rejoice in his state (e.g. in 2.5) and praise her many attractions, while deploring her less endearing characteristics. She is beautiful:

> et quascumque tulit formosi temporis aetas,
> Cynthia non illas nomen habere sinat.   (1.4.7–8)

> *and whatever women the age of Beauty produced, Cynthia does not allow them a reputation to stand on.*

She is *rara* (1.8.42) and his utter absorption in her to the neglect of all others and all prudential counsels is plain:

> ah, mihi non maior carae custodia matris!
> aut sine te vitae cura sit ulla meae?
> tu mihi sola domus, tu, Cynthia, sola parentes,
> omnia tu nostrae tempora laetitiae.   (1.11.21–4)

> *Ah, my protectiveness for my dear mother would be no greater! Or without you would there be any care for my own life? You are my only household, Cynthia, you are my only parents, you are every moment of my happiness.*

Her literary taste is not the least part of her attractions:

> nam mea cum recitat, dicit se odisse beatos:
> carmina tam sancte nulla puella colit.   (2.26.25–6)

> *For when she recites my works, she says she hates rich men: no girl honours poetry so religiously.*

and to her he attributes his own poetic inspiration:

> nam sine te nostrum non valet ingenium.   (2.30.40)

> *For without you my genius has no force.*

The happy times together are rapturously commemorated:

> quanta ego praeterita collegi gaudia nocte:
> immortalis ero, si altera talis erit!   (2.14.9–10)

> *What great joys I gathered this past night: I will be a
> god, if there will be such another.*

Yet the satisfactions are not purely physical:

> quam multa apposita narramus verba lucerna!   (2.15.3)

> *How long we talked with the lamp by us!*

In fact so far from despising her he can claim:

> quod mihi si ponenda tuo sit corpore vita,
> exitus hic nobis non inhonestus erit.   (2.26.57–8)

> *Yet if I must lay down my life on your body, this will
> be no dishonourable end for me.*

4 Propertius constantly sets up an ideal of his own fidelity to
Cynthia, although she herself is notoriously unfaithful to him
even in the *Monobiblos*. His vows of fidelity are reiterated
throughout the first two books; he sees it almost as a moral
matter:

> mihi neque amare aliam neque ab hac desistere fas est:
> Cynthia prima fuit, Cynthia finis erit.   (1.12.19–20)

> *It is not right for me either to love another or leave this
> girl: Cynthia was first, Cynthia will be the end.*

and he considers their relationship to be as binding as any more
conventionally legitimated ties:

> nos uxor numquam, numquam seducet amica:
> semper amica mihi, semper et uxor eris.   (2.6.41–2)

> *A wife will never, a mistress will never lead me away:
> you will always be my mistress, always my wife.*

Even though she rejects him, still he will feel bound to remain
celibate:

> nec domina ulla meo ponet vestigia lecto:
> solus ero, quoniam non licet esse tuum.   (2.9.45–6)

*Nor will any mistress leave her traces in my bed: I shall
stay alone, since I may not be yours.*

Yet no less easy to substantiate is the shattering practice of this
ideal. One elegy (2.22), perhaps not entirely serious, expresses
his weakness for women in general:

> sic etiam nobis una puella parum est.   (36)

So also I find one girl too little for me.

And there is the frustrated attempt, so vividly described in 4.8,
to revenge himself for Cynthia's infidelities by playing her false
with Phyllis and Teia. Propertius' sentiments then are not those
of a lover who sees infidelity as utterly unthinkable, but rather
of a lover who sets up an ideal which is not always lived up to.
And Cynthia seems to recognize this in complaining of *his* possible infidelities (2.20; 3.6.19ff.; 3.16).

5 Jealousy is of course everywhere apparent. Obvious examples are the tirade against the praetor from Illyria (2.16) and
other unnamed rivals (2.9 and 18). General fears of Cynthia's
infidelity, sometimes of a very unreal nature, are constantly in
evidence. When looking at Cynthia asleep, Propertius is afraid

> neve quis invitam cogeret esse suam.   (1.3.30)

lest anyone should force her to be his against her will.

He is jealous of Gallus and Lynceus (1.5 and 2.34), of the
dangers of Baiae (1.11), of the opportunities offered by the
games and temples of Rome. He is delighted when she is in
the country out of harm's way:

> nullus erit castis iuvenis corruptor in agris,
>   qui te blanditiis non sinat esse probam . . .
> illic te nulli poterunt corrumpere ludi
>   fanaque, peccatis plurima causa tuis.   (2.19.3–4,
>   9–10)

*There will be no young seducer in those pure fields, who
by his blandishments will not let you be faithful . . .*

> *There no games can corrupt you, no temples, the main*
> *cause of your sins.*[17]

6 The desire to 'rescue' the beloved which Freud found so
surprising a feature in lovers of this type takes various forms in
Propertius. There is, for example, a concern for her reputation,
to be seen particularly in 2.32.21–2:

> sed de me minus est: famae iactura pudicae
> tanta tibi miserae, quanta meretur, erit.

> *But it matters less about me: the loss to your good*
> *name will be as great, you poor thing, as you deserve.*

The elegies for her safety in time of illness (2.28) cannot of
course be cited as evidence – they would be compatible with
any deep relationship. But the example quoted by Freud of
the lover who wrote tracts to keep his mistress on the path of
'virtue' prepares us for the subtler forms this instinct can take.
A number of Propertius' elegies read like such tracts; their
hortatory character distinguishes them from the poems prompted
simply by jealousy. There are protests against her ways of
dressing and her use of cosmetics, largely because they lead to
or imply moral degradation (1.2; 2.18.23–38). He pleads with
her to remain faithful to him (2.5; 2.16) and warns her of the
possible dangers and penalties (1.8.5–8; 2.5.3–4). And he praises
her when she avoids the temptations of the town by staying in
the country (2.19).

Such concern for her has even subtler manifestations. The
mythological examples which begin elegy 1.3 are Ariadne and
Andromeda (a favourite myth with Propertius). These symbol-
ize very well the protective feelings clearly revealed in lines
27–30:

> et quotiens raro duxti suspiria motu,
>   obstupui vano credulus auspicio,
> ne qua tibi insolitos portarent visa timores,
>   neve quis invitam cogeret esse suam.

17 Cf. also 1.8, 1.13, 2.15, 2.1.47–8, 2.8, 2.24.15–16, 30–3, 2.29, 2.32,
   2.34.1–24, 3.8.33–4, 37–40, 3.19, 4.8.15–16.

> *And when, now and again, you moved and heaved a
> sigh, I froze numb, believing it an omen, lest some vision
> bring you strange fears, or lest someone force you to
> be his against your will.*

But the most striking manifestation of his desire to 'rescue' her
is the strange poem 2.26 (*Vidi te in somnis fracta, mea vita,
carina*). This has many of the marks of a genuine dream.[18]
This is not unexpected, for the dream exactly symbolizes the
desire to 'rescue' the beloved from possible dangers.[19]

Thus all of the traits described by Freud can be adequately
paralleled in Propertius. If this is accepted, much about his liaison with Cynthia becomes clear. It is for example easy to understand why so much of his poetry is openly concerned with the
degrading emotion of jealousy: it was a necessary ingredient in
the relationship. Sometimes indeed Propertius seems aware of
this. The complaisance he shows in 2.32.62 (*semper vive meo
libera iudicio*) is otherwise most surprising. He does not, despite
his jealously, find her infidelities as unbearable as Catullus found
Lesbia's.

The portrait of Cynthia, which varies from the highest praise
to unflattering reflections on her sexual morality, becomes more
explicable. She had to be sexually tarnished for Propertius to
love her, yet she is praised and over-valued for all her other talents and attractions – her beauty, her dress, her culture and
poetic taste. Until his love abates and the scales drop from his
eyes (3.24.2, 6), Propertius was genuinely in love with her and
his writings provide one of the earliest and clearest examples
of this type of Romantic passion. This is not to claim that Pro-

18 Notably the vagueness of the location and the abrupt awakening
when Propertius tries to throw himself from a rock. If it is based
on a real dream, it has of course been considerably added to.
Typical additions would be the comparisons in lines 5–6 and the
poetic ornament of lines 9–10 and 13–16. For the abrupt ending, cp.
Lucretius 4.1020–4.

19 There may indeed be more symbolism discernible in the dream.
The connection with water might point to her maternal aspect
for Propertius, particularly in view of her age and Propertius'
claim, *tu mihi sola parens* (see Freud, n. 12 above, p. 202).
Nevertheless, the straightforward interpretation (which seems
undeniable) is all we require here.

pertius is unique among Roman elegists in his sensibility[20] or to deny his debts to his Greek and Roman predecessors. But what may be justly asserted is that he uses his material to express a coherent attitude to Cynthia and to offer us a consistent picture of himself as a certain type of lover. Unlike Ovid, Propertius, along with Catullus and perhaps Gallus, represents a revolution in sentiment akin to the rise of Courtly Love in the eleventh-century Languedoc, whereas Ovid represents a counter-revolution and a return to more conventional classical attitudes. After Ovid, one must reiterate, there is no elegiac love poetry in the classical period worthy of the name.

The problem of elegy 1.1

If our analysis is correct, it should be possible to elucidate certain general and particular problems in Propertius through our understanding of the character of the lover exhibited in the *oeuvre*. It has been suggested earlier that, given Propertius' particular romantic sensibility and male vulnerability, his Alexandrian interest in mythological themes as a poetic mode of expression would run into certain difficulties in the erotic elegies. With some few exceptions, the Milanion–Atalanta myth, for example, significantly deployed in the opening of Book 1, most classical mythology involving love and passion cast the heroines into the roles of the abandoned or maltreated lover. Even where adultery is in question, the wronged man or god tends to be a *husband* (Vulcan, Theseus etc.), rather than a pitiful and passionate lover. This central fact may account for some of the strangeness of Propertius' use of mythological *exempla*, for the very glancing and obscure implications he has to rely on. (It may also account for the insubstantial and rarely symbolic use of mythology by Tibullus and Ovid when dealing directly with their passion as ill-treated lovers: the *exempla* were not there as they were for, say, fidelity or perverted passion.) This however is a large topic and it is better here to apply the analysis to a more limited problem which is capable of a simpler solution.

20 Se A. V. Rankin, '*Odi et Amo*', *American Imago* 17 (1960) 437–48, for a similar analysis of Catullus' relations with Lesbia.

The opening lines of Propertius' first elegy present precisely such a problem:

> Cynthia prima suis miserum me cepit ocellis
>   contactum nullis ante cupidinibus.
> tum mihi constantis deiecit lumina fastus,
>   et caput impositis pressit Amor pedibus,
> donec me docuit *castas odisse puellas*
>   improbus et nullo vivere consilio.

> *Cynthia was the first who captured lovesick me with her eyes, me untouched before by passionate desires. Then love cast from my eyes their steadfast aloofness and pressed down my head with his feet upon it, until he, the villain, taught me* to hate chaste girls *and live without thought or plan.*

The great and real difficulties of this elegy, in particular of the first eight lines, have gradually yielded to the efforts of critics. But about one phrase at least, *castas odisse puellas* (line 5), there is still no general measure of agreement.[21]

Two explanations of *castas odisse puellas* may be immediately rejected: (1) the interpretation of the phrase as implying that Propertius has turned to common prostitutes in despair (*quaerere viles*) and (2) the various suggestions that the *castae puellae* are the Muses and that he has had to give up poetry. Against the first it may be objected that it is incompatible with line 8 (*cum tamen adversos cogor habere deos*); and also that *furor* would not be the correct description of such a way of living, and finally that it is too much out of key with the mythological example of Milanion; against the second, that this would be a strange way of beginning a book of poems which are positive evidence that Propertius had not come to hate the Muses. Thus we are left with the following possible explanations: (*a*) that the *castae puellae* are virtuous women of some sort, whereas Cynthia is not; (*b*) that they are women who are faithful to their lovers, and Cynthia has rejected Propertius because she al-

---

21   For the literature and the detailed arguments, see my '*Castas odisse puellas*: a reconsideration of Propertius 1.1', *WS* 74 (1961) 92ff.

ready has another lover; or (*c*) that they are women who (for whatever reason) deny sexual favours to their suitors as Cynthia has denied Propertius.

Both (*b*) and (*c*) are open to serious objections. Against (*b*) it may be urged that on the evidence of Book 1 alone Cynthia is not one who would be faithful to any lover – she is certainly unfaithful to Propertius and he reflects that she will be *perfida* in all situations (cf. e.g. 2.9.1–2). Moreover, the tone of the complaints made by Propertius in his unhappy state does not fit this interpretation. He speaks of *ira* (line 28) and of a desire to get away from all women (lines 29–30). In one who has the conventional estimate of fidelity such *ira* is hardly justified; it must be caused by Cynthia's *saevitia*.

(*c*) may be taken in slightly different ways. But such explanations are all open to the criticism that *casta* cannot mean simply a woman who says no in a particular case to a particular suitor (line 36). Furthermore, the natural interpretation of *castas puellas* would exclude Cynthia – she is emphatically not chaste (except perhaps intermittently) and *casta* cannot simply mean *dura* or 'uncompliant' even in its weakest sense. Propertius is summing up a whole year's experience in this opening poem; he is already quite aware of her sexual character and devotes several elegies in Book 1 to expostulating with her for unchastity. Were Cynthia included in the *castae*, it would make nonsense of the feminine character he builds up in the *Monobiblos*. The reader will soon know her for what she is (cf. 1.2.23, *non illis studium vulgo conquirere amantes*), just as Propertius *already* knows her for what she is. Moreover Propertius cares for a good deal more than the satisfaction of desire. He has a high opinion of Cynthia for all her sexual delinquencies and he is jealous of her favours.

Purely philological considerations then exclude interpretations (*b*) and (*c*), but the difficulty about (*a*) may well have been the strangeness of the sentiment when the phrase *castas odisse puellas* is taken literally. The literal interpretation avows openly an emotional attachment to someone who is *incesta*, and an unconventional reaction (*odisse*) to what is generally accepted as a woman's crowning glory, sexual fidelity. But if Propertius is the sort of lover described earlier, then the strangeness of the sentiment vanishes, and we see instead a clear-eyed recognition of Propertius' psychological orientation. He has, for the first time, found himself in love with a woman who has all the qualities requisite to arouse in him the compulsive passions of love and jealousy. And love has taught him to despise what would be naturally regarded as proper love-objects, namely women who would be faithful to their lovers or husbands *(castas puellas)*. These are the sensible choices for anyone who wishes to be happy in love. Hence his advice to other lovers (lines 31ff.). Where love is mutual, with kindness and fidelity as natural consequences, men should be content with their happy situation:

> vos remanete, quibus facili deus annuit aure,
>   sitis et in tuto semper amore pares. (31–2)

> *stay where you are, you to whom the god has given his consent with willing ears, and may you be always equal in a safe passion.*

> hoc moneo, vitate malum: sua quemque moretur
>   cura, neque assueto mutet amore locum. (35–6)

> *this evil, I warn you, avoid: let each man's darling hold him and let him not shift from the love he is used to.*

To leave a long-familiar mistress with whom one is happy to pursue someone who is perhaps another's, and who is, in any case, an unknown quantity, is folly: yet this is what Propertius has done.

Romantic love as a passion is compulsive and irrational: Propertius naturally sees his situation in classical terms, nor could he do otherwise. Love is externalized as Amor and the reproaches a modern man would direct at himself or his emotions are naturally directed against the external forces to which the Roman attributes his helpless plight. For Propertius it is an external and divine power that has robbed him of his former *hauteur* for such women as Cynthia (lines 3–4); thus he sees himself in the grip of *furor*, and it may be noted that modern ways of speaking about love reflect a similar attitude to the stronger passions. The interesting difference between Propertius' and the more conventional classical attitudes to love is the great-

er depth and fidelity of his self-analysis – he is aware that he is
in love with someone who is *incesta*, yet recognizes his inability
to cure himself of this disease. His over-estimation of Cynthia
does not rise to the heights of disbelief in her unfaithfulness
and cruelty. Yet clear-sighted though he is about Cynthia and
his feelings towards her, there are elements in the situation which
he is unaware of. We can see, as Propertius could not, that his
sufferings, his jealousy, his acceptance of Cynthia's evil qualities,
are psychologically *necessary* to him, despite his complaints and
his longing for surcease: his agonies are real, but granted his
nature they are necessary concomitants of his falling in love. The
wise advice he gives other lovers is not advice he could himself
follow. For this is *love*, not a sensual liaison, and in common
with most of the ancient world he is ready to see it as disease.
Cynthia is the first to have infected him with it, as he claims in
line 2: *contactum nullis ante cupidinibus.*

The possible other objections against this interpretation of
castas odisse puellas are of no great weight. It is true that on this
view a slur is cast upon Cynthia, but then much of the *Monobiblos* casts even more specific aspersions on her (e.g. 8 and 15)
and Cynthia, of course, could not justifiably take such offence
as a virtuous woman or more faithful mistress might; although
even the truth can wound. But in any case the mood of the
opening elegy is angry and resentful *(sit modo libertas, quae
velit ira, loqui)*; why should he hesitate to contrast her with more
virtuous women and himself with lovers who are not under the
sway of *improbus Amor*?

How far does this interpretation tally with the myth of Milanion and Atalanta? It could be argued that Propertius' mythological parallels are not always very apt. Obvious examples are
Alphesiboea (1.15.15–16) and the story of the Centaurs and
Pirithous (2.6.17–18), which do not properly illustrate their re-
spective subjects, sexual fidelity and suspicious jealousy. But provided it is understood that only a certain facet of the situation of
Milanion is throwing light on Propertius' relations with Cynthia,
the illustration becomes not unreasonable. The stress is not on
Atalanta's refusing to grant Milanion her favours or accept his
honourable proposal, but on the *sufferings* (*nullos fugiendo . . .
labores*, line 9) he underwent before he could tame his beloved

(domuisse, line 16). Propertius has undergone similar or worse suffering but has not similarly succeeded. The Milanion illustration does not preclude any earlier granting of Cynthia's favours to the poet; the difference is that Cynthia *continues* to maltreat him. The parallel is not between Atalanta's initial refusal to marry Milanion and a similar refusal on Cynthia's part, but between her *saevitia* and Cynthia's. The course of true love has not run smoothly:

> in me tardus Amor non ullas cogitat artes,
>   nec meminit notas, ut prius, ire vias.   (17–18)

> *in my case, sluggish Love thinks up no devices, and forgets to go his familiar ways as before.*

Cynthia, unlike Atalanta, will not be softened and will not reciprocate his passion. So he invokes witchcraft to make her fall in love with him (*et facite illa meo palleat ore magis*, line 22). But if this fails and his passion is hopeless, his friends must try to cure him of his madness.

Elegy 1 then is best taken as an analysis of Propertius' passion and a summary of a year's experience with Cynthia. All the complaints of the elegy will be documented at length in the rest of the *Monobiblos*. It is not the frustrated outcry of a rejected lover, who is later to be accepted by Cynthia, for there is no evidence in the poem that he has not so far been granted her favours at all. With a mistress like Cynthia even the accepted lover may suffer from her *saevitia* and *duritia*, and jealously as well as rejection may bring *amaras noctes* (line 33). But the safety of a reciprocated and equal love, confirmed by time and familiarity (lines 31–2, 35–6), is not for him. Just as the anonymous Pompeian claimed (with Propertius' verse in mind) that a fair beauty had taken away his taste for her darker opposites,[22] so Propertius confesses that his love for an *incesta* had made her opposites, the *castae puellae*, similarly unattractive.

22 *Candida me docuit nigras odisse puellas* (CIL IV.1520).

4
ROMAN CALLIMACHUS

Preliminary considerations

'Properce! . . . quel merveilleux sujet!' wrote Julien Benda in the opening paragraphs of his book.[1] 'Les transformations de l'élégie, l'alexandrinisme à Rome, les écrivains latins au lendemain de la bataille d'Actium ou une génération de la victoire!' A voice stops him: 'Perds-tu le sens? . . . Quoi! tu tiens un auteur dont l'oeuvre est expressément le cri d'une âme, d'une passion, et, au lieu de t'employer de toute ta force à devenir cette âme, à vivre cette passion, tu vas faire de l'histoire littéraire?' His answer to the romantic voice, defending Propertius as a poet of passion, not literature, was: 'mais cette âme est celle d'un poète, cette passion celle d'un homme de lettres. Elle s'exprime dans des formes littéraires.'

I have chosen in these pages to present Propertius first in his political and counter-cultural aspect, because we are nowadays aware that *Make Love, Not War* is primarily a political rather than an erotic declaration. But the critical approach Benda proposed goes also to the heart of Propertius' work and his imaginary interlocutor is simultaneously raising (and stifling) all those doubts about Propertius' genuine passion and 'sincerity' that appear, in various guises, in critical discussions of Propertius' poetry, particularly when focusing on his mythology and aetiology.

Benda's answer, that his passion, however profound, was the passion of a man of letters and a man of his age, which was therefore transmuted in his work, without invalidating its reality or sincerity, would seem a superficial answer to a question rarely raised in post-romantic criticism.

We no longer apply a *simpliste* criterion of 'sincerity', that of

[1] *Properce, ou les amants de Tibur* (Paris 1928) 7ff.

correspondence with fact; we have adopted a saner view of the relation between artistic technique and lyric impulse. The age that revived Metaphysical poetry does not associate only a spontaneous surge of emotion with love poetry. Benda's emphasis on the Alexandrian in Propertius will hardly shock scholars whose main approach to Propertius has been through *Quellenforschung* and the formal analysis of individual elegies. True, there was a time when critics were prone to question, in a naive way, the 'sincerity' of the passion which was the chief subject of Propertius' poetry, to find Propertius artificial, pedantic, and often lacking the direct emotional honesty and involvement that is observable in Catullus. To argue against such doubts by declaring, as did H. E. Butler and E. A. Barber, that 'underlying all there is such fire and vehemence that we can scarcely doubt the general truth of the story that emerges as we read',[2] was, in fact, to adopt the very premises of these hostile (and Romantic) critics. Nowadays scholars have gone back to the salutary principles of some ancient critics, such as Petronius (*Satyricon* 118.6), who distinguish firmly between history and poetry, and thus, by implication, between biographical facts and literary creation. 'Sincerity' for them is a function of style: no specific or necessary connections are to be made between personal poetry and personal experience.[3] The point is obvious with Ovid, but it is also highly relevant to the love poetry of Propertius. The Roman love poets must be judged as individual poets, not as exemplars of a single stream of passionate poetry which becomes progressively more diluted as we move from Catullus to Tibullus, from Tibullus to Propertius, and from Propertius to Ovid. This tradition is not one of diminishing degrees of emotional sincerity and seriousness, but of different ways of writing poetry.

The Alexandrian heritage

'Alexandrianism' is an annoyingly vague term, both historically

---

2 *The Elegies of Propertius* (Oxford 1933), p. xi.
3 See the effective protest made by A.W. Allen, ' "Sincerity" and the Roman elegists', *CP* 45 (1950) 145–60.

and critically.[4] As currently used, it has more connotations than 'Hellenistic', which is not devoid of them. The confusions in the concept derive not only from the many conflicts of poetic principle that one may detect in those poets and scholars regarded as Alexandrian, but also from the critical superstructure that the moderns have erected over the term by the analogous application of it to such periods as the age of Pope or to the work of T. S. Eliot and Ezra Pound. The handbooks tell us that Alexandrian poetry is the Greek poetry written between *c.* 300 B.C. and 30 B.C.; that the name is given this enormous amount of work because its greatest achievements were produced in just over a quarter of a century, in Alexandria and a few other places between 280 B.C. and 240 B.C.; that the spirit of this period permeates, prospectively and retrospectively, all the surviving Greek literature of the period before we reach other periods, almost as hard to distinguish, such as the Second Sophistic. The concept is therefore somewhat dubious. It is perhaps no more useful than the term *Silver Age* (as opposed to *Golden Age*), when applied to Latin literature. What common denominator can we find in such writers as Asclepiades of Samos, Aratus, Apollonius Rhodius, Alexander Aetolus, Bion, Callimachus, Euphorion, Hermesianax of Colophon, Hedylus of Samos, Herodas, Lycophron, Meleager of Gadara, Menecrates of Ephesus, Moschus, Nicander, Parthenius, Poseidippus of Samos, Phoenix of Colophon, Philitas, Rhianus, Simias of Rhodes, Theocritus, and Zenodotus of Ephesus (the list is by no means exhaustive)?

The writers of this period supposedly turned away from the grand old genres to more polished minor forms. We are told, particularly with reference to Callimachus and his contemporaries, that epic, lyric, and tragedy were considered too ambitious for the new age and different types of literature were called for; hence the invention of new forms and the desire for innovation and experiment. But the plain fact is that epic continued to be written by Alexandrian poets, not least by Apollonius Rhodius, who was perhaps the most ambitious and

---

4 See the remarks of W. V. Clausen, 'Callimachus and Roman Poetry', *GRBS* 5 (1964) 193ff.

successful since his work invited direct comparison with Homer. Tragedy, too, which was surely the second most prestigious genre to come down from the classical age, continued to be written. We even know of a Pleiad of tragedians at the Alexandrian court of Ptolemy Philadelphus (285–247 B.C.). Only lyric poetry of the Pindaric type, which was already in decline by the end of the fifth century B.C., seems to have had little representation among the many experiments and revivals that we find in so-called Alexandrian literature, a fact of significance for the study of Horace.

It would be easy to enumerate the new forms which were prominent or invented in the years after 300 B.C. Many of the favoured forms were simply improvements on or developments of forms that had been used by someone or other, in the classical and pre-classical periods. Epic, whether mythological or historical (and the distinction was not always as clear to the Greek mind as it is to us), tragedy, and epigram continued; as did didactic poetry with Hesiod as the great exemplar of the genre, although it flourished in this period as never before. Aristophanic comedy seems to have been a unique phenomenon in the ancient world, but New Comedy continued well into the period, and Plautus and Terence both testify to its vitality, even where we do not have the works of those who continued writing in this form. It would seem then that there are precious few forms that one might accept as truly Alexandrian, and even then their beginnings may be paralleled in one way or another in the archaic and classical ages: narrative elegy, the so-called 'epyllion' (a short, oblique poem on an epic theme or motif), hymns, non-tragic iambic poetry, and so on. Perhaps a claim of true novelty might be made for *paignia* and *techno-paignia*, which produced such masterpieces as poems which could be engraved on, or represent such things as, an axe, a pipe, or an egg.

Given this paltry haul of really innovative forms that we may attribute to the Alexandrian period, can we point to a totally different spirit that distinguished this literary period from the periods before 300 B.C.? Alexandrianism is supposedly dominated by a thrust for knowledge and reflects the enormous progress being made in natural science, mathematics, and philology. Historical and literary research, because of its importance in the great libraries, became also a dominant mode in poetry itself. Hence the fondness for artificial dialects, archaism, and learned and scientific allusion, as well as the metrical experimentations and the recombination of older forms.[5]

It is however in the attempt to penetrate to the *essence* of Alexandrianism that the handbooks become more obscure. On the one hand, we are told of a retreat to the study, or rather the library, to concentrate on aetiological and lexical research; on the other, we are told of urban realism in the *Mimes* of Herodas and escapist pastoralism in the *Eclogues* of Theocritus. On the one hand, we are told of the Alexandrians' interest in the softer side of human life as seen in Apollonius' treatment of Medea and in the erotic epigrams of the period; on the other, we are told of their delight in such versified treatises as Aratus' *Phaenomena*. The confusion seems to arise from trying to impose on a period comprising several centuries a set of literary characteristics which may be used to contrast that period with the great eras that went before it. It is an attempt to impose scholarly order on what might be regarded, more charitably, as creative chaos.

Instead of proposing, then, a neat definition of Alexandrianism, in order to examine its effects on Roman literature, and particularly on Propertius, I prefer to single out from this chaotic post-classical period a number of significant themes and movements which had their effect on Roman poetry in the generation immediately before Propertius and which became dominant influences on Propertius' art.

Callimachean principles

It was the school of Callimachus, if we may even call it a school rather than a certain critique and practice, which was the important focus for the transmission of so-called Alexandrianism

---

5 See now R. Pfeiffer, *History of Classical Scholarship* (Oxford 1968) 87–170; the literature on Alexandrian poetry is immense, but good summaries of standard views for the English reader are provided by A. Lesky, *A History of Greek Literature* (London 1966) 694–9; and T.B.L. Webster, *Hellenistic Poetry and Art* (London 1964) 39ff.

to Rome. Despite Ovid's patronizing description (*quamvis ingenio non valet, arte valet, Am.* 1.15.14), Callimachus had an
enormous effect on both his Greek contemporaries and also on
the teachers who promoted his influence among the poets of
the late Republic and the early Empire, not to mention the
poets who went to him and his canon directly.[6] Admittedly an
admiration for Callimachus and the poets he approved of did
not preclude much radical oversimplification, perhaps even dis-
tortion, of his theory and practice. Even his opponents were
prone to this. To the generation after Propertius, Callimachus
became known simply as the prototype of the scholarly pedant,
who tended to cast aspersions on Homer and destroy poetry.[7]
Nevertheless if we take Cicero as an early anti-Callimachean
and Horace and Persius as the next hostile critics of note, we
will see that Callimachus' not undisputed influence on Roman
poetry lasted about a century.

What, then, was Callimachus' critical theory and poetic practice? We may reconstruct it from our assessment of the poets
whom he admired, or with whom he was associated, in literary
history — most notably, Philitas, Theocritus, Euphorion, Heraclitus, and the poets he attacked, such as Asclepiades of Samos,
Poseidippus, and the proto-Alexandrian, Antimachus.[8] It is a

6 The most obvious example of this is Catullus with his translation
of the *Coma Berenices*. Ennius was influenced by Callimachus
and yet chose to write in a way which later adherents to
Callimachean principles would probably not have approved.
See in general, W.V. Clausen, *art. cit.* above, note 4.
7 Cf. *A.P.* 11.321, 322, 347; Mart. 10.4; Juv. 7.232ff.
8 His most useful statements are to be found in Fr. 1 Pf. (with the
Scholia); *Hymn* 2.105ff.; *Epigrams* 9, 10, 29, 30, 53, 60. The
following *testimonia* in Pfeiffer (vol. II, pp. xcviii ff.) are also
important: 22, 25 (= AP 11.275), 25a (= Mart. 10.4.9ff.), 26,
27, 28, 37, 55 (= *Catalepton* 9.61ff.), 56 (= Hor. *Epp.* 2.2.91ff.),
57 (= Prop. 2.1.39f.), 58 (= Prop. 3.1.1ff.), 62 (= Ov. *Am.*
1.15.13f.: Ovid, I believe, is here boasting of his own
extraordinary facility, which he equates with *ingenium*!), 63
(= Ov. *Am.* 2.4.19f.—another Ovidian boast, this time, of his
sophistication!), 65 (= Ov. *Rem. Am.* 381f.), 66 (Ov. *Rem. Am.*
759f.), 67 (= Ov. *Trist.* 2.367f.), 69 (= AP 11.321), 70 (= AP
11.347.5f.), 71 (= AP 11.322), 72 (= AP 11.130), 73 (= Statius,
Silv. 1.2.252ff., who associates Philitas, Callimachus,
Propertius, Tibullus and Ovid), 75 (= Mart. 4.23), 76 (= Quint.
Inst. 10.1.58, who ranks Callimachus first and Philitas second of

pity we do not have more of his *Dunciad,* the *In Telchinas,* which opened his *Aetia.*

What is clear from the evidence is that, first, Callimachus sets himself against the long epic poem on standard mythological themes. To say that Callimachus was opposed to all writing on epic themes, in the age in which he found himself, is too simplistic a view. The surviving fragment of his that describes the advent and defeat of the Gauls in their attack on Delphi (Fr. 379 Pf.) makes this clear, as does the questionable nature of the evidence of his quarrel with Apollonius of Rhodes who, we are told, wrote his *Argonautica* in defiance of the Callimachean pronunciamentos: 'A big book is a big bore' (Τὸ μέγα βιβλίον ἴσον ἔλεγεν εἶναι τῷ μεγάλῳ κακῷ, Fr. 465 Pf.) and 'I hate epics about Troy and Thebes' ('Εχθαίρω τὸ ποίημα τὸ κυκλικόν, *Epig.* 28). It would seem that Callimachus banned epic as a proper modern form without exception and that Apollonius, to judge from his work, simply thought that epic could be written, provided one handled it in an Alexandrian, that is, non-Homeric and non-heroic way. Vergil, perhaps with some misgivings, took the same view.

Callimachus was not opposed solely to epic. Contrary to the verdicts of many whom Callimachus might have claimed as his allies in this controversy, he also disapproved of the *Lyde,* the elegiac mythological poem to his dead mistress, written by that proto-Alexandrian, Antimachus who, we may note, also wrote a *Thebaid.* In Callimachus' view, contrary to that of Plato, Antimachus had not yet developed the proper artistry (Λύδη καὶ παχὺ γράμμα καὶ οὐ τορόν, Fr. 398 Pf.); his learning and language were not yet properly under control nor refined enough. Nor were Callimachus' strictures directed simply against length *per se.* Aratus' *Phaenomena* was no brief poem. The question was one of treatment, style, and subject. Callimachus wrote his famous

the Greek elegists), 77 (= Plin. *Epp.* 4.3.3), 78 (= Lucian. *de conscrib. hist.* 57, who berates Parthenius, Euphorion, and Callimachus for their wordiness in handling mythological subjects), 87 (Callinus, Mimnermus, Philitas and Callimachus are rated by Proclus as the best Greek elegists), 88 (Propertius, Tibullus and Gallus are rated the main Roman elegists to be regarded as followers of Callimachus and Euphorion).

'epyllion', *Hecale*, but also the *Aetia*, to refute the contentions of his opponents that he could not write a long poem.

The *Aetia*, as far as we can judge from its extant fragments, was more like the *Cantos* of Ezra Pound than Milton's *Paradise Lost*. It was a sometimes discontinuous poem, which perhaps expressed best his preoccupations and art. Ovid, who tended to overdo all things, but who was, nevertheless, the last of the committed neo-Alexandrians or neo-Callimacheans, prides himself on producing the real *carmen perpetuum,* where the linked episodic and variegated style would not be subject to Callimachean objections and might indeed fulfil, as perhaps he felt Callimachus had not, Callimachean objectives. If Callimachus finally found Apollonius Rhodius wanting, despite his attempt to produce a truly Alexandrian epic, then too Ovid must have found the *Aeneid* also wanting and his *Metamorphoses* was the response, based upon models such as Nicander's *Heteroeoumena* and Parthenius' own *Metamorphoses.*[9]

It is when we attempt to define the treatment and the style of the poetry that Callimachus favoured that we have to turn to a variety of inferential evidence and analogies. Obviously he favours the more artistic and refined developments of the poetic art which he discerns in the elegies of Philitas, who might be regarded as the real founder of Callimachean poetry. He sees merit in the elaborate epigrams of such poets as Heraclitus, whose 'nightingales' he praises so deftly in the epigram on his dead Carian friend; in the town and country idylls of Theocritus (cf. *Id.* 7.35–40), the Hesiodic *Phaenomena* of Aratus, and similar genres. Would he have approved also of the *Alexandra* of Lycophron and the poems of Parthenius?

To talk of a learned or polished style is not enough. It is rather the creation of an individual – indeed, artificial – poetic mode which would be utterly unlike the hand-me-down, unpondered Homeric diction in which a myriad contemporary or

9 For a new defence of Apollonius' and Vergil's belief that epic could be written in a way that did not run counter to Callimachean critical theory, see T.M. Klein, 'The role of Callimachus in the development of the concept of the counter-genre', *Latomus* 33 (1974) 217–31. Catullus, Propertius, and Ovid, however, persisted in their more rigidly Callimachean position.

near-contemporary writers told and retold the standard myths
of the epic cycle. This willingness to create an artificial dialect
and to utilize Ionic, Doric, and Aeolic forms indiscriminately
had various motives. Perhaps foremost was the desire to produce
on the reader an impression of self-conscious artistry, which
sometimes might take the form of irony and sophisticated objectivity, but it facilitated also verbal sonority,[10] thus combining, in Ezra Pound's terms, *melopoeia* with *logopoeia*.[11] (The
natural sonorousness of Latin and the pressure for the standard-
ization and purification of written Latin inhibited the elegiac
poets from following their mentors in this respect.)

It was not the length of a poem but rather the *treatment* of
the subject matter that was at issue. It was a matter of *leptotes*
as opposed to *semnotes*. It was a matter of a dispute between
those who thought they could mechanically write on the themes
that the Cyclic poets had treated before them and those who
thought that a new style, perhaps new forms, were more appropriate to the modern age. Thereafter poets whose purposes
were thus suited could attack epic and propose elegy (somewhat defensively and apologetically) as the only type of verse
worth writing. Poets who thought they could manage epic in
the new style, like Apollonius (and Vergil at the end of his
career), went on their own way.

These writers were, in fact, destined to predominate. Each
generation thereafter of Latin literature produces writers of epic
on mythological or historical subjects: Statius, Valerius Flaccus,
Silius Italicus – the list is endless, even though so few survive.
But the undercurrent of criticism from the Callimachean circles
left its imprint on the literary opinion even of the later imperial
period. The hostility of Martial and Juvenal to grandiose or
exotic subject matter is well known, but Persius, for example,
seems equally opposed to the standard epic themes and to
neo-Callimachean techniques, and it is to be noticed that his
criticism of Greek models attacks the subjects of the cyclic epic
writers and not only the more *recherché* metrical practices of
the Callimachean school. Callimachus not only wanted unfa-

10 See B.A. van Groningen, *La poésie verbale grecque* (Amsterdam
1953), 28f.
11 See below, pp. 147–58.

miliar myths to be used as the subject of poetry, but he also wished the poems utilizing this material to be constructed in a different way from the standard epic approach. Callimachus insisted that mythological poems should have a modern centre or a modern technique. His desideratum was the out-of-the-way myth which might incorporate recent history or might serve to explain the origins of certain rituals. In the construction of such poems the technique to be used was to be non-linear, oblique, and learnedly allusive. In the *Hecale* (Frr. 230–377 Pf.), for example, he takes the standard mythical theme of Theseus' labours, culminating in his slaying of the Bull of Marathon; he concentrates, however, not on conventional heroic action, but on the realistic description of Theseus' reception by Hecale the night before the action. For other writers of 'epyllia', it was not the journey for the Golden Fleece, but the sad loss of Hylas; not the labours of Heracles, but his childhood, that were appropriate subjects for poetic representation.

It would appear then that, besides the conscious delight in words and allusions, the most important ingredient in Callimachean *leptotes*, to be discerned in the *Hymns* and in the *Lock of Berenice* (Fr. 110), is a distancing, an irony verging on humour, which Propertius was slowly to develop in his own poetry. The best description of this quality is Pound's term: *logopoeia*, a self-conscious mode, which we may best analyse when we deal directly with Propertius' style.

The neoteric tradition and its enemies

With so many of his Greek and Roman predecessors lost or fragmentary, it is difficult to speak with certainty of the exact nature of their influence on Propertius. One may surmise, however, that Propertius learnt from the Neoterics, from Catullus and his like-minded contemporaries (e.g. Valerius Cato, Calvus, Cinna, and Varro), the freedom to indulge in autobiography, in the analysis of his relationship with Cynthia, particularly in his first book. The habit of addressing his friends in these elegies, especially prominent in the first book, might also be seen as part of the influence. The impersonality of Greek elegiac practice is, on the whole, absent except in those areas where Alexandrian mythological interests take control.

One important distinction between Greek and Latin poetry is the strong preponderance in the latter of the personal and the autobiographical. The letters of Plato are very impersonal compositions indeed when set beside the letters of Cicero. The major original component the Romans brought to the writing of elegy was the complete involvement of their personality and their individual circumstances, however transmuted by art. This tendency grows between Tibullus and Ovid. Various subtle judgements may be made about the depth and degree of this personal exposure in the three elegists, but even if we dislike the extroversion and monotony, clearly visible in the works written in exile, Ovid exposes more of himself than any Alexandrian poet. Those critics who feel that Propertius' personal feelings are all too often overlaid by the frigid mythology he derives from his Roman and Alexandrian predecessors should not be dismayed by how *much* mythology there is in Propertius, but rather recognize how comparatively *little* there is in terms of the tradition within which he worked. We no longer accept the dichotomy in Catullus between the learned Alexandrian and the heartbroken romantic poet, if the premise upon which this was based was the clear distinction in the *oeuvre* between personal poetry and Alexandrian 'epyllia'. We are now aware that the spontaneous personal poetry contains just as much art as the more formal set pieces. But in Propertius we have, in almost every elegy, a fusion of Latin individualism and Greek technique, at least until the fourth book which presents a special problem.

The first book is very much under the influence of Catullus although the personal poetry, however artistically projected, and the Alexandrian technique are well blended. It seems to me that in the middle stage of Propertius' development, that which covers all the poetry between Books 1 and 4, Propertius was trying to incorporate more of Alexandrian practice into his verse than he could in Book 1, partly by reaching out after other subjects and partly by enriching his poetic technique.

Propertius gives us a select and untrustworthy list of his predecessors in Roman love elegy (2.34.85ff.):

> Haec quoque perfecto ludebat Iasone Varro,
> Varro Leucadiae maxima flamma suae;

> haec quoque lascivi cantarunt scripta Catulli,
>   Lesbia quis ipsa notior est Helena;
> haec etiam docti confessa est pagina Calvi,
>   cum caneret miserae funera Quintiliae.
> et modo formosa quam multa Lycoride Gallus
>   mortuus inferna vulnera lavit aqua!

We may paraphrase:

> *Varro, too, toyed with these themes when his transla-*
> *tion of the* Argonautica *was completed, Varro, the great*
> *passion of his dear Leucadia; the pages of the lascivious*
> *Catullus also have poems of this sort and through them*
> *Lesbia is more famous than Helen herself; the work of*
> *the learned Calvus, too, admits these things when he*
> *writes of the death of poor Quintilia and later we know*
> *from the writings of Gallus about the beautiful Lycoris*
> *how many heartaches he took beyond the grave with*
> *him.*

Catullus, Calvus, and Varro were all born about 83 B.C. and belong therefore to an earlier generation of neoteric writers. None of them is recognized by Quintilian as an elegist in our sense; only in Catullus can we recognize the first gropings towards the form as we define it. We may assume that such verses as were written on their mistresses were in epigrammatic form, derived from Alexandrian epigram, or in the case of Calvus, an elegy, not of the type we associate with Propertius, but the standard elegy on the death of someone: in this case, his mistress or wife. Cornelius Gallus (70 B.C.–27/26 B.C.) is, however, a bridge between that generation of love poets and the generation of Tibullus and Propertius and we may surmise that he is the first of the elegists, as recognized by Quintilian, to analyse, in some way or another, the shifting relationships he enjoyed or endured during his affair with Cytheris, before the actress abandoned him for Antony.

It is becoming clear that the influence of Parthenius of Nicaea, the Greek poet captured during the Third Mithridatic War, was considerable. He gained his freedom in Italy in 73 B.C. and presumably was able to give a closer reading of the principles of

Callimachus to his Roman associates. He enjoyed a high esteem
for his elegiac poetry and from the few fragments that survive it
may be surmised that his influence on Cornelius Gallus was more
than just the material from mythology that he gave him.[12] If we
can trust Quintilian's judgement that Gallus was *durior* than the
other elegists, this quality may be due to his clinging more closely
to the practice of his literary mentor. For the later elegists the
principles of the Greek elegiac couplet had to be refined and
adapted to the genius of the Latin language. Elisions and polysyllabic endings in the pentameter, as well as certain hexametric
practices, fell gradually out of favour.

Propertius then, somewhat defensively, as we shall see later,
aligns himself with this tradition of Roman poetry. But just as
Callimachus has his contemporary enemies such as the two Di-
onysii, Asclepiades, Poseidippus, Praxiphanes, and presumably
others,[13] so the earlier followers of Callimachus, the *poetae novi*,
had their critics and their own *bêtes noires*. There is no need
to postulate a school; it was simply the cultural influence of such
writers as Callimachus and Euphorion which made the Neoterics
despise long-winded annalistic poets such as Volusius (Cat. 36.1,
20; 95.7), and abandon certain time-honoured metrical practices
(e.g. the elision of final *s* before an initial consonant, Cic. *Orator*
161) in favour of more *recherché* Greek practices (cf. Cic. *ad
Att.* 7.2). Cicero and others of his generation disapproved of
them for their disregard of the extant Latin tradition of public
poetry (Ennius' *Annales*, for example) and the whole epic–
tragic emphasis of early Latin literature. This tradition, with
Lucilian satire, as Horace sourly observed, still enjoyed great
respect even in Augustan Rome (*adeo sanctum est vetus omne*

12 It is interesting to observe that of Parthenius' mythological
stories about the miseries of love, dedicated to Cornelius Gallus,
five of the thirty-six involve the theme of the woman who betrays
her country or king and then, instead of gaining the reward she
desires, comes to an untimely end. This, of course, is the theme
of Propertius' 4.4, the story of Tarpeia. Four other stories in
Parthenius are concerned with the personal betrayal by a wife or
lover of her husband or equivalent. In all cases, the guilty female
party comes to a bad end. Parthenius also handled the myth of
Scylla in his *Metamorphoses*, another popular myth in Propertius
(2.26.53; 3.12.28; 3.19.21; 4.4.39).
13 See Schol. Flor. ad Fr. 1 (Pfeiffer).

poema, Ep. 2.1.54). But even among the moderns disagreement prevailed.

Few literary controversies, of course, are solely over critical principles: personalities, jealousy, life-style, even political attitudes, tend to intrude with the *genus inritabile vatum.* Of Horace's circle, clearly Varius Rufus had no objection to writing epic and tragedy as well as elegy; Vergil, after a firmly Alexandrian beginning, spent his last years on the *Aeneid* – without entirely abandoning his Callimachean interest in aetiology. To Horace, however, the Callimachean purists were an affront and his dislike was doubtless shared by others.[14] His sneers at elegy in particular (*Od.* 1.33), but also at neoteric poetry in general (*simius iste|nil praeter Calvum et doctus cantare Catullum, Sat.* 1.10.18–19) were but the negative aspect of his exhortations to his poetic friends to tackle grander and more public-minded themes (*os magna sonaturum*). He insisted, with Neoptolemus of Parium and other Peripatetic critics, that poetry should combine utility and pleasure (*omne tulit punctum qui miscuit utile dulci, Ars Poetica* 343); his ex-slavish adherence to Augustan ideals, and to the emperor himself, naturally expressed itself in a demand for public poetry as against the private themes of the elegists whom he scolds. The task of the *vates*, a term that took on a new life at this period[15] and which was meant to emphasize the role of the poet as spokesman of (and to) the community, was to celebrate the state and its rulers; to heal the wounds left by the Civil War; and to memorialize the discomfiture of Rome's enemies. The lesson Horace learnt from Callimachus was how to do this laboriously, effectively, and well.

Horace was consequently Propertius' enemy (see pp. 12ff. above) and a large part of the hostility must have been based on critical and ideological grounds. Propertius was the most prominent articulator of Alexandrian doctrines, the self-professed

---

14 Horace's critical principles may be deduced from *Sat.* 1.4; 1.10; *Ep.* 2.1; and the *Ars Poetica. Od.* 1.1; 1.6; 1.33; 2.9; 2.12; 2.16; 3.1; 3.4; 3.30; 4.2; 4.3; 4.6; 4.9; 4.15 provide further, if oblique, information. In general, see C.O. Brink, *Horace on Poetry, Prolegomena to the Literary Epistles* (Cambridge 1963) and the literature there cited.

15 See J. K. Newman, *The Concept of Vates in Augustan Poetry, Collection Latomus* 89 (Brussels 1967).

Roman Callimachus, the most successful of the second generation of *poetae novi*. Gallus was in disrepute, besides being a military man, and Tibullus was a friend both to Horace and to Messalla, on whose military staff he had served. He could be allowed to cultivate his own garden without more than an amicable rebuke. But Propertius' airs were perhaps more difficult to tolerate.

Defences and counterattacks

The tension one may discern in Propertian poetry is partly due to this pressure. The *poetae novi* of the Republic were defiant and iconoclastic in their newly-learned poetic creed. Catullus attacked Julius Caesar and the *Annals* of Volusius with equal vigour. A few deprecatory terms, *lusus, nugae*, etc., were justified by Callimachean precedent and were, in any case, balanced by the use of such terms as *facetus, venustus, urbanus, lepidus* with their proud connotation of 'civilized'. Propertius, however, had to resist not only the standard pressures of Roman common sense about matters erotic, Roman ambition for military, political, or legal glory, but in addition the ideological and critical pressures of the new regime and its poetic champions, such as Horace. A willingness to allow the Roman Alcaeus his meed of honour was not enough; such tolerance would be rebuffed. It is possible that both parties here had an uneasy feeling that the other might be right. The common aim, after all, was to produce great and lasting art, but success in this was immediately judged by current public opinion and Propertius' *Monobiblos* had been more successful than Horace's three books of Odes. Nevertheless Horace, whatever he had learnt from Alexandrian artistry, stood firmly in the Latin tradition of public poetry: the poetry of the battlefield, the forum and the classroom, not the poetry of the library, the study, and the *boudoir*.

One *riposte* for Propertius and poets like him was to appropriate the concept of *utile* and profess himself a teacher also, whose didactic works, recommended reading at least for the love-lorn and for passion's apprentices, were more 'useful' than epic and other lofty genres:

> plus in amore valet Mimnermi versus Homero   (1.9.11);

me legat assidue post haec neglectus amator
   et prosint illi cognita nostra mala   (1.7.13–14);

quem legat expectans sola puella virum   (3.3.20);

'ut per te clausas sciat excantare puellas,
   qui volet austeros arte ferire viros.' (3.3.49–50).

Another response was to proclaim oneself part of a genuine tradition, which included not only Callimachus and other like-minded Alexandrian poets, but also the *poetae novi* (2.34.85ff.). Even Vergil could be co-opted for this purpose (2.34.81–2). This allowed the poet not only to boast of the fame already gained by his chosen predecessors, but also to lay claim to a similar immortality for himself, an immortality that can be compared with that of even the greatest epic writer:

nec non ille tui casus memorator Homerus
   posteritate suum crescere sensit opus.
meque inter seros laudabit Roma nepotes:
   illum post cineres auguror ipse diem.   (3.1.33–6)

Homer, the chronicler of Troy's fall, felt his work's reputation grow with the lapse of time. And Rome will praise me in later generations: I myself prophesy that day after my death.

But such apparently defiant claims, a commonplace anyway in most ancient poetry *(non omnis moriar)*, could not hide the fact that the elegist was producing art for art's sake – or art for the heart's sake. An art, moreover, that had to be described in the terminology of *levis, deductus, gracilis, tenuis, Philiteus* as opposed to *gravis, durus, rotundus, Pindaricus*, and so on. True, Callimachus had been able to elevate *leptotes* to a critical pinnacle, but social and literary conditions at Alexandria differed radically from those now prevailing in Rome. The most versatile defence therefore for Propertius was the elaboration of the *recusatio*, the poet's apology for writing as he wishes to write.

The grand refusal

Although the poetic motif of professing inability or unwillingness to handle certain themes and styles probably predates the Alexandrian age, it was Callimachus, particularly in his prologue to the second edition of the *Aetia,* who produced the paradigm that could be adapted for many different literary forms, whether satire, elegy, ode, epistle, eclogue or other.[16] The refusal to write on a certain topic or in a particular genre could be allegedly prompted by the poet's own inability or reluctance; by the too great importance of the theme; or by the greater capacity and availability of other talents. The poet might be dissuaded or influenced by a god, a Muse, an astrologer, or his own mistress. The refusal might be couched in the imagery of highways and byways; broad rivers and small streams; oceans and shore-lines; deep draughts of poetic water and sips from unpolluted springs; mighty throats and tiny whistles: but the message was the same:

> sed neque Phlegraeos Iovis Enceladique tumultus
>   intonet angusto pectore Callimachus,
> nec mea convenient duro praecordia versu
>   Caesaris in Phrygios condere nomen avos.
> navita de ventis, de tauris narrat arator,
>   enumerat miles vulnera, pastor oves;
> nos contra angusto versantes proelia lecto:
>   qua pote quisque, in ea conterat arte diem.

(2.1.39–46)

> *But Callimachus, with his narrow views on poetry, would not be thundering out the skirmishes of Jupiter and Enceladus on the Phlegraean fields, and my talents also will not be capable of tracing Caesar's family back to his Trojan forebears in lofty verse. A sailor talks of weather, a ploughman of bulls; a soldier counts over wounds, a shepherd his sheep. So, despite it all, I tell of lovers battling in a narrow bed. Let the cobbler stick to his last.*

It is part of my thesis that the *recusatio* is an integral part of Propertius' poetry and is used by him in more subtle and pervasive ways than by any other contemporary poet. One need only look at the transformations it undergoes in the *oeuvre*. With Callimachus, it is simply a matter of defending his literary views

16 The main collection of evidence and previous literature on the subject is that of W. Wimmel, *Kallimachos in Rom: Die Nachfolge seines apologetischen Dichtens in der Augusteerzeit, Hermes Einzelschriften* 16 (Wiesbaden 1960).

124   *Roman Callimachus*

and obliquely denigrating his critics. With Horace, it is a matter of shucking off importunate demands and hewing to his own chosen style of handling public themes. With Propertius, it becomes a whole new genre, that simultaneously displays his poetic abilities, rejects Augustan pressures, and defines the true nature of his art.

The *recusatio* takes various forms in Propertius and elements of the form may be found in poems that are not strictly focused around the motif.[17] The obvious examples, of course, are those that follow Callimachean models (e.g. Fr. 1.19–28 Pf.):

μηδ' ἀπ' ἐμεῦ διφᾶ τε μέγα ψοφέουσαν ἀοιδήν
τίκτεσθαι· βροντᾶν οὐκ ἐμόν, ἀλλὰ Διός.
καὶ γὰρ ὅτε πρώτιστον ἐμοῖς ἐπὶ δέλτον ἔθηκα
γούνασιν, Ἀπόλλων εἶπεν ὅ μοι Λύκιος·
'........... ἀοιδέ, τὸ μὲν θύος ὅττι πάχιστον
θρέψαι, τὴν Μοῦσαν δ' ὠγαθὲ λεπταλέην·
πρὸς δέ σε καὶ τόδ' ἄνωγα, τὰ μὴ πατέουσιν ἅμαξαι
τὰ στείβειν, ἑτέρων ἴχνια μὴ καθ' ὁμά
δίφρον ἐλᾶν μηδ' οἶμον ἀνὰ πλατύν, ἀλλὰ κελεύθους
ἀτρίπτους, εἰ καὶ στεινοτέρην ἐλάσεις.'

And do not look for a loud-sounding song to come from me. It is not for me to thunder, but Zeus. For when first I placed a tablet on my knees, Lycian Apollo said to me: '(Dear) poet, feed the sacrifice to be as fat as possible, but, my good fellow, keep the Muse slender. And this too I tell you: tread where the traffic does not go; do not drive your chariot in the same tracks as others or along a broad road, but down unworn paths, though you drive a narrower way.'

Elegy 3.3, for example, depicts Propertius about to embark on an epic about Roman history, the sort of project he knew Vergil was engaged on:

Visus eram molli recubans Heliconis in umbra,
    Bellerophontei qua fluit umor equi,
reges, Alba, tuos et regum facta tuorum,

17 The main 'apologies', sometimes ironic or defiant, for his life style or poetic work are : 1.7; 2.1; 2.10; 2.34; 3.1–3; 3.5; 3.9; 3.17; and 4.1.

tantum operis, nervis hiscere posse meis;
parvaque tam magnis admoram fontibus ora,
    unde pater sitiens Ennius ante bibit . . .
cum me Castalia speculans ex arbore Phoebus
    sic ait aurata nixus ad antra lyra:
'Quid tibi cum tali, demens, est flumine? quis te
    carminis heroi tangere iussit opus?
non hic ulla tibi speranda est fama, Properti:
    mollia sunt parvis prata terenda rotis;
ut tuus in scamno iactetur saepe libellus,
    quem legat exspectans sola puella virum.
cur tua praescriptos evecta est pagina gyros?
    non est ingenii cumba gravanda tui.
alter remus aquas alter tibi radat harenas,
    tutus eris: medio maxima turba mari est.'

*I dreamt I was lying in the soft shadow of Helicon,
where the water of Bellerophon's horse flowed and I
dreamt that I could sing of the kings of Alba and their
deeds, a mighty task. I had moved my dainty lips to
the mighty fountains whence Father Ennius had thirst-
ily drunk . . . when, looking at me from the Castalian
grove, Apollo, leaning on his golden lyre at the entrance
to a grotto, spoke these words: 'What have you to do,
madman, with such a river? Who ordered you to handle
a subject of heroic poetry? There is no fame to be
hoped for in this for you, Propertius: small wheels must
roll over soft fields; so that your little book will often be
tossed on to a table, when a girl, reading it, is waiting
alone for her man. Why has your page been carried
away from its prescribed course? The boat of your talent
must not be weighted down. Let one oar ply the water,
let the other graze the sand, and you will be safe; the
biggest commotion is on the high sea.'*

What genius he has is for love poetry and later Calliope confirms
this by his baptism in the water of Philitas.

The difference between Callimachus and Propertius should be
noted. Callimachus' instructions from Apollo are direct: the god
offers a particular conception of art. In Propertius' poem, the
loftiness and value of heroic poetry are not criticized, but Pro-

pertius is told that it is *not for him*. The apparent (or ironic) defensiveness is far more prominent. Similarly in the elegies to Maecenas (2.1 and 3.9), it is not the worth of the epic genre or the important historical subjects proposed which is decried, but Propertius' own poetic capacity or his inspiration, which is Cynthia:

> ingenium nobis ipsa puella facit.

This defensiveness, in contrast to the defiance of Callimachus and Catullus, is due, of course, to specifically *Augustan* pressures. Propertius knew what Maecenas would have requested of him and was aware of the place usurped in the literary consciousness by Vergil and Horace, the poets of the Establishment, whether they liked it or not. He moves ambiguously therefore between apology and pride; between apology for his dedication to love-poetry (2.1, 3.9 etc.) and pride in his poetic allegiances and expected fame (3.1 etc.); between hankerings after more grandiose themes (including such sanctioned subjects as αἴτια) and a determination to stick to his admired predecessors and his neoteric topics and forms.

His friends who write epic and tragedy, such as Ponticus (1.7) and Lynceus (2.34); his fellow poets, such as Vergil and Horace; Maecenas, Augustus, and the spirit of the times, push him one way. Apollo, Calliope, and Horos; Callimachus, Philitas, even Mimnermus; his predecessors in Latin erotic elegy, such as Catullus and Gallus, push him another. The struggle is a prominent feature of the poetry, but I have no doubt, contrary to the accepted view that Propertius succumbed to 'what the age demanded',[18] where the victory went.

18 The accepted judgement about the relationship between Propertius' public and private themes seems indicated by one of the latest studies of his work, where the patriotic note is put even earlier in the *oeuvre*. According to this view, Propertius is 'tout le contraire d'un autonomiste ou d'un opposant à la romanisation . . . le poète passe de la poésie érotique du début du livre II, des professions de foi amoureuse à la poésie de la grandeur impériale . . . Properce participe à la sensibilité nationale, au désir de la "propagatio imperii" . . . est divisé entre son goût de la poésie, et de la vie personelle, d'une part, et sa fierté de citoyen, de l'autre' (J.-P. Boucher, *Etudes sur Properce. Problèmes d'inspiration et d'art* (Paris 1965) 111, 113, 114, 116).

The nature of Propertius' Art

Through the *recusatio*, then, Propertius defends his art and his private themes against imperial pressures and real or imagined critics. Other poets had used the *recusatio*, of course, even while writing poetry perfectly consonant, politically, with the spirit of the times (notably Vergil, cf. *Ecl.* 6.1–12; and Horace, cf. *Od.* 1.6). Usually the intention was to avoid writing an epic. Propertius' surface modesty about his current poetic status and the audience he will attract is balanced by an underlying confidence about his ultimate vindication through time. We must now ask what was Propertius' conception of his poetry as he developed its range and complexity. To invoke the ideals of Callimachus and Philitas, to speak of the polished style, or poetic delicacy, are not enough: Horace too owed a debt to Callimachean precepts. Some superficial characteristics may be dealt with briefly. The *ordonnance* and balance of elegies within each book, except for our present Book 2, are exemplary: complementarity and *variatio* are achieved even if Propertius, as in Book 1, had to turn out specific material to secure them.[19] Diptych arrangement, although never so obvious as with Ovid's 'Cypassis' elegies (*Am.* 2.7 and 8), may be seen in the arrangement of 3.4 (*Arma deus Caesar . . .*) and 3.5 (*Pacis Amor deus est . . .*) and 4.1, where Propertius' boasts and Horos' warnings may constitute, in effect, two separate elegies which were meant to be read together.

As regard metrics, Maurice Platnauer's study[20] of the elegists' verse practices allows us to define the differences between Propertius and his Greek and Roman predecessors and contemporaries.

Although, as we have seen, Propertius came to conform, more or less, to Augustan practice in his pentameter endings, yet he is, in many ways, closer to Catullus (and, presumably, Gallus) and thus, ultimately, to Greek practice. This of course does not indicate lack of care; in some ways, as with Catullus, his verse is the stronger and more varied for it. He uses more non-caesural or quasi-non-caesural lines than either Tibullus or Ovid (46 or just over 2% by comparison with Tibullus' 13 which is just under

---

19 See O. Skutsch, 'The structure of the Propertian *Monobiblos*', *CP* 58 (1963) 238–9, on the arrangement of the *Monobiblos*.
20 M. Platnauer, *Latin Elegiac Verse* (Cambridge 1951).

2%, and Ovid's 11, a mere 0.1%). He has six examples of non-caesural hexameters with a trisyllable forming a bacchius in the third and fourth feet, a type found in Catullus (e.g. 68.39). It is noticeable also that his practice becomes more and more Callimachean in certain ways between Book 1 and 4. For example, whereas Greek, because of its plethora of words beginning and ending in short open vowels, offers many examples of hexameters with a weak caesura in the third foot (e.g. Callimachus in *Hymn* 5, *The Bath of Pallas*, has 57%), only Tibullus tried consciously to lighten the line in this way (20%); nevertheless, Propertius' practice shows a small increase: Book 1, 3.4%; Book 2, 4.4%; Book 3, 6.3%, and Book 4, 7.4%. Similarly diaeresis after the fourth foot, the so-called 'bucolic diaeresis', was a matter of indifference to the elegists, but there is the greatest percentage of it (57%) in Book 4. Again, Hermann's Bridge, the avoidance of caesura after the fourth trochee, a practice consistently observed by Callimachus and usually followed by Catullus in his longer poems, was generally respected by Propertius in his earlier work (Book 1 has only 7 violations, whereas Book 4 has 29). Since in pre-neoteric elegiac epigrams the Bridge is rarely found, this may be seen as a conscious imitation of Callimachus, dropped later.

Spondaic hexameters, derided by Cicero as marks of neoteric poetry (*Ad Att.* 7.2.1), were usually limited to writers of hexameter verse. Nevertheless, unlike even Callimachus, Catullus (with two exceptions) and Tibullus, Propertius allows himself the liberty of seven lines of this type (1.13.31, 1.19.13, 1.20.31, 2.2.9, 2.28.49, 3.7.13, 4.4.71), generally incorporating Greek words such as *heroine*.

No doubt subtle analyses could turn up further evidence of Propertius' imitation of Callimachean or mediated Callimachean verse practice, but, as I shall argue, given the differences between the Latin and Greek languages, such minor effects are not to the point. It was the spirit of Callimachus' poetic philosophy that Propertius wished to imitate. Still, it can be affirmed that Propertius followed neoteric practices in the main, although using the notorious spondaic hexameters sparingly and gradually moving from the Callimachean, indeed generally Greek, practice of frequent polysyllabic endings in the pentameter to the Augustan norm of dissyllabic endings. As I have suggested above, this, like the growing disregard of Hermann's Bridge, may have been under the influence of Tibullus and other Augustan elegists.[21]

Propertius' 'Alexandrianism' (in the above sense) may be seen also in his language: the fondness for Greek geographical and mythological epithets; the admixture of the colloquial, even un-poetic, words with neologisms, diminutives, archaisms and poetic words; the allusions to, and echoes of, his Alexandrian models, his Latin precursors, and his Augustan contemporaries (Vergil, Horace, etc.); and his innovative syntax: all combine to produce something approximating in Latin the artificial dialects that the Alexandrians used so freely.[22]

Although it was not central to his art, Propertius, like Catullus and Tibullus, experimented with minor Alexandrian themes and motifs. In Book 1 we find the elegiac equivalent of an 'epyllion' (20), the story of the rape of Hylas, Hercules' companion, a minor episode in the *Argonautica* cycle, which was similarly treated by Theocritus, *Idyll* 13. A variant of the *paraclausithyron* is found in 16: here the door reports the complaint of the locked-out lover inveighing against the cruelty of his mistress. 1.21 is a funerary epigram.

2.12 and 2.31 are ecphrastic exercises;[23] the first perhaps describing a real, or imaginary, depiction of Eros; the second describing, somewhat perfunctorily, the new portico of Apollo on

21 It would be interesting to know the effect, if any, of Ovid's verse practice on Propertius.

22 See H. Tränkle, *Die Sprachkunst des Properz und die Tradition der lateinische Dichtersprache, Hermes Einzelschr.* 15 (Wiesbaden 1960), and B. Axelson, *Unpoetische Wörter* (Lund 1945).

23 These prose or verse descriptions, or comments, on works of art or sculpture have a long history, going back to Homer's description of the Shield of Achilles (*Il.* 18.483ff.). Vergil's counter was the illustration of the story of Troy in Dido's temple (*Aen.* 1.453ff.). But the pages of the Palatine Anthology, whether of an early or late date, not to mention Petronius and Martial, are cluttered with such descriptive poems, generally praising the realism of the painter (or sculptor) or narrating the story limned. None of these efforts, in my opinion, can compare with W.H. Auden's *ecphrasis* on Pieter Brueghel's *The Fall of Icarus*. I do not except Propertius 2.12 from this stricture and it should be added that, according to Athen. 13.562c and Quint. 2.4.26, Eros the winged god was also a conventional literary theme.

the Palatine, dedicated in 28 B.C., although it is given a more personal touch by shaping it into an excuse for the poet's tardy arrival. 3.17 is a hymn to Bacchus, although it is far shorter than any of Callimachus' surviving hymns. 4.5 is a genre piece, equally Alexandrian, describing a drunken bawd: Herodas' first mime is the extant prototype.

But these Alexandrian essays are peripheral to Propertius' central concerns. Two aspects of his debt to the Callimachean tradition are somewhat more significant: his use of mythological themes and his poetic investigations of rituals, customs, and religious names, in the manner of the *Aetia*.

Mythology

Mythology in classical authors, apart from such well known myths as the stories of the Trojan War and the misdeeds of Aphrodite, is largely a stumbling block for the modern reader. For contemporary poetry it is becoming, with many exceptions, an outmoded convention, now that its tremendous revival in romantic literature and Victorian poetry is past. Indeed to what precise extent it was of value to English literature is a critical question of some interest. We cannot conceive an English literature without it, and there are of course considerable successes to its credit: Chaucer's *Troilus and Criseyde*, for example, as well as a host of minor triumphs like Tennyson's *Ulysses* and Yeats' *Leda*, where mythology assumes a symbolic function as it rarely did in Roman and Greek mythological writing or in the pseudo-classical pastoral and mythological narratives of the seventeenth and eighteenth century. On the other hand the amount of sheer bad poetry to be found on classical myths, as on many other topics, is vast. But so inert is the acceptance of mythological subjects (not of course *symbolism*) as a *donnée* in most ancient poetry that we fail to notice how, in the main stream of Latin literature, there runs a current of protest from poets against the use of trite Greek myths as poetic material.

Catullus falls into two parts: allegedly his best, most Roman, work is more or less free from mythology. And under the principate, when political conditions most encouraged such literary self-indulgence, we have the protests of Persius, Martial, and

Juvenal to remind us of the real strength of the Latin tradition. Even Lucan tried to get away from the divine machinery of epic, presumably reacting against the Vergilian imitation of the quite differently conceived Homeric gods, and it is interesting to note Lucan's reported approval of Persius' satires, compared to which, he said, his own and similar work was only trifling (Suet. *Vita Persi*). Nor must it be forgotten that as a religious reality the Olympian gods led in Rome a precarious existence at the best of times; not even Vergil could do much for them. The use of mythology in Latin literature appears at times to be a means of escape; it provided easy and safe subjects for the ambitious or facile versifier, and of course the admiring, but sometimes un-intelligent, use of the Greek literary tradition was partly to blame. There was indeed from the very beginnings of Roman literature an attempt, self-consciously continued, to use specifically Roman subjects for epic poetry instead of the Greek historico-mythical subjects. The *Annals* of Ennius, the *Pharsalia* of Lucan, and the *Punica* of Silius Italicus are obvious representatives of this tra-dition, just as the use of historical Roman figures and almost contemporary historical events is to be found alongside the con-tinued use of the Greek myths in the poetry of Vergil, Horace, and Propertius. But the spell of mythology is to be seen nowhere better than in Silius, who undoes, with the reintroduction of Vergilian divine machinery, the critical revolution Lucan had tried to effect. This is not to say that better poets, such as Statius and even the younger Seneca, could not use classical myth to comment indirectly on their own times.

The poetic use of mythology may be classified in three ways. There is its use as subject matter, whether for narrative, dra-matic, or semi-dramatic purposes. There is its symbolic function, perhaps the most significant, for here its peculiar and primitive value as a sort of para-scientific explanation of the world has en-dowed it throughout its long history with a vital power which goes far beyond the simple interest of the myths as stories. Freudian or Jungian psychology may explain the fascination, but its patent presence makes it still a powerful source of poetic symbolism. Even though it can never again be so powerfully used to express a view of the universe as it was by Pindar and the Greek tragedians, yet Teiresias, 'old man with wrinkled dugs', is an acceptable poetic symbol, even in a predominantly non-mythological period of poetry. Finally, there is the use of myth as poetic ornament: that is, all the uses of mythical subjects and personages for simile, comparison, description, and image.

It would be little of an exaggeration to say that mythology in straight narrative poetry began to lose ground with the decline of heroic saga and epic. The Alexandrian narratives with their obscure mythical stories and Alexandrian secondary epic rarely produced great poetry, because they could not draw upon symbolic sources. Without these sources the material is cut off from life and the interest lies only in the treatment. Vergil, for example, is a great poet, yet the *Aeneid*, at least on the divine level, is something of an impressive failure, except where, here and there, his material comes to life (as in Book 4 where it has a universal and representative theme and Dido and Aeneas cease to be mythical personages and become persons in a general human situation) or when he fuses mythology and symbolism (as in Book 6). But these parts reveal something of the poverty of the rest. Catullus is a genuine poet, but his longer Alexandrian poems on mythological subjects, despite interesting technique, are not what we admire in him today. His strength lies in the Italian tradition of satire, invective, and the poetry of life and passion. And it is Catullus' refusal to clog his most personal poems with mythological allusions that largely produces that impression of tortured sincerity; it is as though he were too pained to think of mythological comparisons. Catullus is an interesting case. He was tempted by Alexandrian models into certain long narrative mythological poems; these untrodden areas of mythology naturally lack for us the psychological reverberations which the great mythical poems have. The equivalents in Propertius are the aetiological Roman legends of Book 4. But Catullus limits himself in this respect (a critical decision), whereas in Propertius the use of mythology extends much further. The interest in myth characteristic of Alexandria is obviously at work. Mythology is extensively used as ornament and becomes one of the stock series of themes through which the elegists triumphantly expressed their personal individuality. 'Ornament' here is not a pejorative term; it is meant to include such legitimate parts of poetic practice as simile and illustration. But there is in such a use of myth a seductive temptation; it can lead to unnecessary and unassimilated ornamentation, the nonfunctioning image, the laboured and unilluminating simile, and the forced conceit. It becomes a substitute for thought.

Distinctions, then, must be made about the use of mythology in ancient poetry as much as in modern. Propertius frequently manages to use mythological situations symbolically, a fairly rare distinction which he shares with Horace and Vergil. Myth becomes a language in which he can talk of his poetic aims and methods. Not infrequently he succeeds in fusing erotic mythology with his own situation and thus effectively adds a third dimension to his affair with Cynthia (e.g., in 2.29a). Propertius is enchanted with the mythological landscape in which he can set Cynthia and her poet. Mythology is used to idealize her, just as Ovid in Book 1 of the *Ars Amatoria* can use the myth of Pasiphae and her unnatural passion for a bull to degrade women in general, in accordance with more 'classical' attitudes. But Propertius is often accused of an unselective padding with mythical illustrations which add, as far as we can see, little or nothing to a poem's poetic logic and in fact distract considerably from its development. Propertius 2.8 offers a paradigm almost: love caused suffering for mythological figures x and y, so why should I not suffer? In some of the worst examples the list of mythological similes could be detached from the poem to the poem's improvement.

The unreality of the detail, which was arguably unreal in some degree to the Roman audience also (witness Martial 4.49), has to be seen in terms of Alexandrian theory. Mythology *is* a stumbling block to the modern reader and means little, detail by detail: some of the stories are frivolous, barbarous, obscene, or dull. But they were generally familiar to, and accepted by, the Roman reader as they are not with us. Propertius could, by a mere name, bring a whole story before his reader's mind; this is not so for us. Propertius took the use of mythology in poetry as a *donnée* from his Alexandrian models. As far as we can see, Greek erotic elegy, even when dedicated to a living or dead mistress (Mimnermus' *Nanno*, Antimachus' *Lyde*, Hermesianax' *Leontium*) tended to be descriptive narrative retailing the sad fates of heroines. Propertius, however, worked his mythological *exempla into* his personal elegies. So I would reiterate that we should be surprised not at how much Propertius overlays the subjective personal elements in his poetry, but how *little* he does so by comparison with his models, whose devotion to obscure mythology was notorious. Of course, the paucity of mythological themes, however *recherchés*, involving a love-struck male subservient to a dominant female might partly account for this and also for Propertius' own adaptations of male–female myths to fit his own situation. The mythology Propertius inherited was, as we observed earlier, fundamentally patriarchal. It should also be noted that only a few of his myths are obscure and that instead of ranging further and further afield for his mythical comparisons, generally offered us in catalogue form (e.g. 1.3.1–6; 2.14.1–8), he returns again and again to his favourite myths.[24] Only rarely, however, is the story elaborated beyond a very few lines. It was not for mythological learning, then, that he went to Callimachus and Philitas, although he saw that as one element, to be combined with the poetic symbols of Apollo, the Muses, Mount Helicon, and the Pegasean spring, which would give his poetry the Callimachean texture he was seeking as the Augustan heir of neoteric poetry.

Aetiology and the problem of Book 4

For all Propertius' professed adherence to Callimachean poetic canons, we find no essays in aetiology until Book 4. This is not to say, of course, that only after the break with Cynthia did he need to find a new type of subject. The elegy on Vertumnus (4.2), for instance, has two polysyllabic pentameter endings (in the space of six lines) and a normally avoided hexameter ending (*tela caduca*, line 53); it is therefore reasonable to surmise that it belongs to an earlier date than much of the material in this last book. Thus this last book presents a crucial problem, since it is generally regarded as Propertius' concession to Augustan

24 For example, references to Andromeda number 4; Antiope 5; Ariadne 3; Briseis 4; Danae 3; Helen 7; Medea 7; Penelope 7. The characteristics common to these heroines are, of course, abandonment in one way or another; fidelity in extreme circumstances; and fame.

pressures. As Syme remarked: 'even Propertius was not un-
touched by the patriotic theme, or the repeated insistances of
Maecenas. For all his dislike of war, he could turn away
from his love and lover's melancholy to celebrate with fervour,
and with no small air of conviction, the War of Actium, or to
plead in solemn tones for the avenging of Crassus.'[25] And Book 4
is regarded by many as his compromise between the demand for
patriotic poetry and grander themes and his Callimachean principles. According to this view, he began the first sketches of a
Roman *Aetia*, represented by elegies 2, 4, 9 and 10 of this book.
This was discontinued, or left unfinished, and rightly, critics
imply, since these elegies have met with almost uniform dis-
favour. Now we may admit at once that poems explaining, sometimes wrongly, the origins of Roman names or rituals are not
much to our modern taste – how few didactic poems are! It is
therefore worthwhile to consider these poems with some care.

Elegy 2, on the god Vertumnus, is light in tone; so light indeed
that it might seem hardly more than a humorous exercise, were
it not for the facts that the statue of Vertumnus was located
at the end of the Vicus Tuscus; that the god is Etruscan and
proud of it (*Tuscus ego: Tuscis orior*); and Propertius alludes
bitingly to Rome's conquest of Etruria (line 4). The humour is
restored by the god's remark that there are only six lines left to
get through and the passer-by hurrying to the lawcourts need
not worry about the delay as the end is in sight:

> sex superant versus: te, qui ad vadimonia curris,
>   non moror: haec spatiis ultima meta meis. (57–8)

An even more obvious example is to be found in elegy 9, where
Hercules, a traditionally humorous subject, is the hero. What
are we to think of a demi-god who pleads for a drink of water
from a fountain reserved for women by saying:

> 'mollis et hirsutum cepit mihi fascia pectus,
>   et manibus duris apta puella fui. (49–50)
>
> *A soft brassière held my hairy breast and for all my
> horny hands I was a deft girl?*

25 *Roman Revolution*, pp. 466–7.

In the first 16 lines of the poem Propertius treats of the legend of Cacus' theft of Hercules' oxen, a subject handled with all aetiological seriousness by Vergil in *Aeneid* 8.184–305. Propertius, however, for most of the poem concentrates on a feature of the rites of the Ara Maxima which both Vergil and Ovid (*Fast.* 1.534–86) pass over discreetly: the exclusion of women because the priestess of the Bona Dea denied him water. It is this *aetion* which occupies Propertius for the next 50 lines. The levity of the treatment may be seen in the dialogue between the priestess and Hercules; he boasts of his achievements, tries to cajole and calm her fears by recounting his feminine as well as his masculine achievements, then finally he loses his temper. He gets the water and pronounces his curse. There is, it is true, a tendency, visible also in the Vertumnus elegy, for this lightness of touch to become purely verbal in the manner of Ovid (e.g. *fessos fessus et ipse*, line 4; *furem . . . furis*, lines 13–14; *bis mihi quaesitae, bis mea praeda, boves*, line 18).

Elegy 4.4 also involves a woman. Here Propertius recounts the tale of Tarpeia, formally to explain the origin of the ancient name of the Capitoline Hill, one prominent rock of which was still called *saxum Tarpeium* in Propertius' day. Hardly an obscure *aetion*, as versions of the story are to be found in Livy, Varro, Dionysius of Halicarnassus and Plutarch. Characteristically, Propertius' version differs from the other versions in making Tarpeia act out of love for Tatius, not greed for gold. Probably this elegy comes closest to the Alexandrian and post-Alexandrian narrative elegies about the fates of various heroines. It bears some resemblance in this respect to the story of Herippe, as retold by Parthenius (8) after Aristodemus of Nysa. In the story of Polycrite, also retold by Parthenius (9), the heroine suffers a similar fate to Tarpeia. The stories of Pisidice (21) and Nanis (22) also concern the betrayals of cities by love-sick girls. It was clearly a popular theme in neoteric poetry, Scylla being another example, treated by both Vergil and Ovid and recalled by Tarpeia herself (39–40).

Most of the poem is concerned with Tarpeia's love-lorn state, 34 central lines being a self-justificatory monologue; the actual action is briefly disposed of. The story was perfectly suited to Propertius' talents as a love elegist, but, despite a few lines of perfunctory condemnation (17–18, 89–92), it was hardly an episode from Roman history calculated to inspire public spirit or moral fervour in the reader. In effect, the story was chosen for its neoteric interest, not its patriotic implications.

4.10 might be an example of combining the Callimachean mode with patriotic Roman subjects. But, as we have seen earlier (pp. 43f. above), the choice of Jupiter Feretrius and the *spolia opima* at this period involved a highly tendentious topic and one scarcely calculated to please the emperor. His Etruscan sympathies are made quite plain once more.[26] The winning of the *spolia opima* by Romulus, Cossus, and Claudius were presumably three very stirring events in Roman history: Propertius disposes of them in 39 lines, leaving the poem far shorter than the average for Book 4. After the ambiguity of 4.1, to which we shall return, the opening lines should perhaps be read with some scepticism:

> Nunc Iovis incipiam causas aperire Feretri
>   armaque de ducibus trina recepta tribus.
> magnum iter ascendo, sed dat mihi gloria vires:
>   non iuvat e facili lecta corona iugo.

> *Now let me expound the origins of Jupiter's title 'Fere-trius' and tell the story of three sets of armour taken from three generals. It is a great road I climb, but ambition gives me strength: a garland from a low height is no pleasure.*

These then are the aetiological elegies from Propertius' pen: the first (4.2) a slight and amusing exercise on an *Etruscan* deity, whom Varro (*L.L.* 5.46) described as *deus Etruriae princeps*; the second (4.4) the conversion of a famous episode in Roman history that demonstrated Jupiter's benevolence towards Rome into a neoteric theme on the vagaries of love; the third (4.9) an amusing treatment of the aftermath of the Cacus–Hercules story,

---

26 Note particularly:
>   heu Vei veteres! et vos tum regna fuistis,
>   et vestro posita est aurea sella foro:
>   nunc intra muros pastoris bucina lenti
>   cantat, et in vestris ossibus arva metunt . . .
>   di Latias iuvere manus, desecta Tolumni
>   cervix Romanos sanguine lavit equos. (4.10.27–30, 37–8)

These must be numbered among Propertius' most moving lines. His deliberate deviation from the presumably standard account in Livy was to stress the Etruscan king's bravery.

involving Hercules once more with an obdurate woman; and the fourth (4.10) a pointed reopening of a delicate question about the *spolia opima*, supposedly settled in 29 B.C. (Dio C. 51.24), and incorporating an elegiac lament over the slaying of Lar Tolumnius, king of the Veii, by A. Cornelius Cossus.

A small haul then for those who would see Book 4 as Propertius' capitulation to the demands of 'the patriot game'.

There are of course several possible explanations for the un-Horatian or un-Vergilian character of these aetiological elegies, for all their lack of appeal to us. Perhaps they are poor pieces which Propertius himself would have regarded as unsatisfactory, but which an editor included in Propertius' last, and posthumous, book. Possibly Propertius, who was at this period producing, or selecting, such elegies as 4.3, 5, 7, 8, and 11 for this last book, was unable to tell his good work from his bad. In this case, however, we would expect more aetiological elegies (of whatever quality) to back up the promises of 4.1.57–70 (*sacra deosque canam et cognomina prisca locorum*).[27]

We must, therefore, turn from the aetiological elegies, to the other poems of Book 4 to see if the riddle of Propertius' intentions can be solved. The solution will not be found, naturally, in such Alexandrian exercises as 4.5, amusing though the treatment of the drunken old bawd is. The heavy Callimachean apparatus of Greek adjectives, mythological allusions, and even two polysyllabic pentameter endings, indicate that this is a genre poem, written somewhat earlier perhaps than the rest of the book.

Propertius' intentions in Book 4

I suggest that Book 4, far from being a concession to Augustan pressures, is in fact Propertius' ultimate *recusatio*.

27 I somewhat favour the emendation *deos* for *dies*. Propertius does not even *date* the rituals of the Ara Maxima; Ovid at least tells us that they occurred in January. In Book 4, two gods (Vertumnus and Jupiter Feretrius) and a demi-god (Hercules) are celebrated; the origins of one feature of the Ara Maxima rituals are given; and an aetiology for the *saxum Tarpeium is* perfunctorily offered. Dates, however, are noticeably absent.

The interpretation of the introductory elegy is obviously crucial to this thesis. On my reading the elegy has to be taken at its face value, namely, as a *recusatio* like 3.3, 3.9, and others. Let us look, therefore, a little more closely at the poem. Propertius is addressing an unnamed visitor to Rome:

> 'Hoc quodcumque vides, hospes, qua maxima Roma est,
>   ante Phrygem Aenean collis et herba fuit;
> atque ubi Navali stant sacra Palatia Phoebo,
>   Evandri profugae concubuere boves . . .' (4.1.1–4)

> *'Whatever you see here in mighty Rome, stranger,*
> *was just grassy hillside before Phrygian Aeneas came,*
> *and where the Palatine, sacred to Apollo, god of sea*
> *battles, now stands, there the wandering cattle of Evan-*
> *der mounted one another . . .'*

Propertius, from his vantage-point overlooking the heart of Rome, next describes what he imagines the various sites of now prominent buildings and landmarks were like in prehistoric times. There is considerable stress on the story of Troy, Aeneas, and the Julian house, as well as on some of the later events of Roman history of the type described by Vergil in the *Aeneid*, particularly in Book 6.

> huc melius profugos misisti, Troia, Penates;
>   heu quali vecta est Dardana puppis ave!
> iam bene spondebant tunc omina, quod nihil illam
>   laeserat abiegni venter apertus equi,
> cum pater in nati trepidus cervice pependit,
>   et verita est umeros urere flamma pios.
> hinc animi venere Deci Brutique secures;
>   vexit et ipsa sui Caesaris arma Venus,
> arma resurgentis portans victricia Troiae:
>   felix terra tuos cepit, Iule, deos;
> si modo Avernalis tremulae cortina Sibyllae
>   dixit Aventino rura pianda Remo,
> aut si Pergameae sero rata carmina vatis
>   longaevum ad Priami vera fuere caput:
> 'vertite equum, Danai! male vincitis! Ilia tellus
>   vivet, et huic cineri Iuppiter arma dabit.' (39–54)

It was well done when you, O Troy, sent your fleeing household gods here; ah, with what good auguries the Trojan fleet put to sea! Already at that time the omens promised well that the gaping belly of the Wooden Horse had done no hurt to those ships, when the frightened father hung from his son's neck and the flames shrank from burning those pious shoulders. From this came the heroism of Drusus and the axes of Brutus; and Venus herself brought us the martial prowess of her Caesar, by carrying here the victorious arms of Troy resurgent. Fortunate the land that took in your gods, Iulus; if indeed the tripod of the shuddering Sibyl by Avernus' shore pronounced that the rural site must be hallowed by Remus, watcher of the Aventine, or if the inspired words of [Cassandra] the prophetess of Pergamum to long-lived Priam, long after fulfilled, were truly said: 'Turn back your Horse, Greeks! You conquer to your own peril! The Trojan land will live and Jupiter will give arms to these ashes.'

By inviting comparison with Vergil, Propertius is advertising that his new project will be as ambitious as any epic, despite the difference of poetic mode. He now tells us what he plans to do:

> optima nutricum nostris lupa Martia rebus,
>   qualia creverunt moenia lacte tuo!
> moenia namque pio coner disponere versu!
>   ei mihi, quod nostro est parvus in ore sonus!
> sed tamen exiguo quodcumque e pectore rivi
>   fluxerit, hoc patriae serviet omne meae.
> Ennius hirsuta cingat sua dicta corona:
>   mi folia ex hedera porrige, Bacche, tua,
> ut nostris tumefacta superbiat Umbria libris,
>   Umbria Romani patria Callimachi!
> scandentes quisquis cernit de vallibus arces,
>   ingenio muros aestimet ille meo!
> Roma, fave, tibi surgit opus, date candida cives
>   omina, et inceptis dextera cantet avis!
> dicam: 'Troia, cades, et Troica Roma resurges'

et maris et terrae longa pericla canam;
sacra deosque canam et cognomina prisca locorum:
    has meus ad metas sudet oportet equus.   (55–70)

*O she-wolf of Mars, best of nurses for us, what a city
grew from your milk! For I would endeavour to tell the
tale of the city in reverent verse: alas that the music of
my song is low-pitched. But whatever the stream (of
poetry) that shall flow from my small talent, all of this
shall be at the service of my country. Let Ennius crown
his work with a ragged wreath; you, Bacchus, must give
me leaves from your (more delicate) ivy, so that Umbria
may swell with pride because of my book, Umbria, the
country of the Roman Callimachus! Whoever sees the
citadels towering out of the valleys there, let him measure the walls in terms of my genius. Rome, applaud!
It is for you the work commences! Fellow citizens,
grant me your favouring prayers and let the bird of
good omen sing over what I now begin! I shall start
with 'Troy, you will fall and as Trojan Rome, you will rise
again!' and I shall sing of the wearying dangers on sea
and land; and I shall sing of rituals and gods and ancient
local names: these are the goals my horse should sweat
to reach.*

The tension between ambition to produce a Callimachean equivalent of Vergil's (and other) epics, an aetiological poem or series
of poems to Rome's greater glory, and the conventional and
disingenuous doubts about his poetic ability and the power of
his chosen Muse is deliberately resolved by his proud boast of
being the Roman Callimachus, who brings such glory to his
native Umbria. The ambiguity about which *patria* his talents
serve, visible in lines 60 and 64, is surely deliberate.

  In the continuation of the poem, which 1b certainly is,
whether we regard it as a separate elegy (diptych construction)
or an abrupt and dramatic discontinuity in a very long programmatic elegy, the mysterious astrologer Horos now breaks
in. Horos plays the part earlier sustained by Apollo and Calliope and warns him to return to love elegy and the life that
goes with it:

'Quo ruis imprudens, vage, dicere fata, Properti?
    non sunt a dextro condita fila colo.
accersis lacrimas cantans, aversus Apollo:
    poscis ab invita verba pigenda lyra.   (71–4)

'*What is all this foolish rush, Propertius, you wanderer,
to sing of destiny. The threads are forming on an ill-
omened spindle. You are inviting tears by this song;
Apollo has turned his back on you. You are demanding
strains you must regret from a reluctant lyre.*'

The astrologer now gives his and his science's credentials to
reinforce his warning (75ff.). He finally moves on from his
anecdotes to Propertius' horoscope and recapitulates his life and
how he came to be a poet:

'hactenus historiae: nunc ad tua devehar astra;
    incipe tu lacrimis aequus adesse novis.
Umbria te notis antiqua Penatibus edit:
    mentior? an patriae tangitur ora tuae?
qua nebulosa cavo rorat Mevania campo,
    et lacus aestivis intepet Umber aquis,
scandentisque Asisi consurgit vertice murus,
    murus ab ingenio notior ille tuo.
ossaque legisti non illa aetate legenda
    patris et in tenues cogeris ipse lares:
nam tua cum multi versarent rura iuvenci,
    abstulit excultas pertica tristis opes.
mox ubi bulla rudi dimissa est aurea collo,
    matris et ante deos libera sumpta toga,
tum tibi pauca suo de carmine dictat Apollo
    et vetat insano verba tonare Foro:
"at tu finge elegos, fallax opus: haec tua castra!
    scribat ut exemplo cetera turba tuo.
militiam Veneris blandis patiere sub armis,
    et Veneris pueris utilis hostis eris."
nam tibi victrices quascumque labore parasti,
    eludit palmas una puella tuas:
et bene cum fixum mento discusseris uncum,
    nil erit hoc: rostro te premet ansa suo.

illius arbitrio noctem lucemque videbis:
   gutta quoque ex oculis non nisi iussa cadet.
nec mille excubiae nec te signata iuvabunt
   limina: persuasae fallere rima sat est.'   (119–46)

'So much for old stories: now let me move on to what is
in your stars; get ready to face fresh causes for tears.
Ancient Umbria produced you from a distinguished
household. Do I lie? Or do I hit on the place of your
native country? Where the misty Bevagna bedews the
hollow plain and the Umbrian lake is warm with its sum-
mery waters, and the walls of climbing Assisi rise from
the hill-top, walls the more famous through your genius.
You gathered (from the pyre) the bones of your father,
too early to be gathered at that age, and you yourself
were reduced in your property: for though many bullocks
grazed your fields, the hateful surveyor's rod sheared
away your cultivated land. And when the golden amulet
of childhood was removed from your still young neck
and the toga of a free man was put on before your
mother's household gods, then Apollo dictated a few
verses to you from his poetic store and forebade you to
thunder speeches in the mad Forum, saying: "No, you
must write love elegy, a deceptive genre. This is your
battlefield, so that the other writers may profit from your
example. Serve out your time in Venus' army. The fight-
ing is sweet and you will be a good opponent for her
Cupids." For whatever palms of victory you have ac-
cumulated by your labour, one girl still eludes your
palms: even when you do fortunately break into bits the
hook fixed in your chin, this will be nothing: her gaff
will still hold you with its curving spike. By her decision will you see night and day: not even a drop will fall
from your eyes except at her command. Not a thousand
vigils nor a thousand campings on her doorstep will help
you: a chink is enough for a woman persuaded to betray you.'*

The poem ends with a warning against the astrological sign
of Cancer, a sign usually associated with wealth. Given the

context of Cynthia's infidelities, Propertius' reduced circumstances and his many complaints of her avarice in earlier books,
the warning makes an appropriate, if to us somewhat *recherché*,
conclusion to the poem. The high-flown style of Propertius'
announcement (which may be seen in his earlier *recusationes*)
and the oddities of the astrologer and his threats do not, as
some have thought, militate against the interpretation that Propertius is once more refusing, under the thin pretext of super-
natural guidance, to commit his talents to the glorification of
Augustan Rome and its supposedly divine and fateful origins.
Horos does not represent the critics who think that Propertius
can only write love poetry and whom Propertius intends to
prove wrong.[28] For, to judge from the specimens of aetiological
elegy in Book 4, which in any case are hardly *sacra deosque*
yet, Propertius would *not* have proved them wrong, and it is
hard to believe that Propertius was such a poor judge of his
work that he thought he could. What he will have proved is
that pressure on him, however delicate, to write on public
themes (*publica carmina*, in Ovid's words) was fundamentally
mistaken. If this interpretation is correct, then the whole of
Book 4 may be seen as an elaborate and ironic *recusatio*. The
best elegies are among the private poems, say 7, 8, and 11; the
public poems are either deliberately light or subtly subversive.
Propertius' claims in earlier books to be a love-poet and Horos'
warnings in this book are thus vindicated. Nor can Propertius
be accused of ingratitude or contumacy.

Of course it is not impossible that Horos' speech (1.71ff.)
was added to the opening elegy, or written later as a second
poem to be taken in close conjunction with the opening poem
of the book. In that case one could assume that Propertius
began his aetiological enterprise hopefully enough, but found
either his inclinations or his talents inadequate to the still un-
congenial task. But whether Propertius knew it would turn out
this way or simply made the best of a bad job, the result would
be the same.

The notorious elegy 6 on the battle of Actium (*Sacra facit*

28 As is argued most recently by P. Fedeli, *Properzio: Elegie libro
IV* (Bari 1965) 69ff.

vates), which constitutes a main ground for alleging that Propertius succumbed to Augustan pressures to write court poetry, may now be seen perhaps in a different perspective. This poem has been almost universally condemned as frigid by critics[29] and it has been used as an argument that Propertius' true strength lies in his 'sincere' and impassioned love poetry. But if one takes the poem in the context of the whole book, one is left with an uneasy feeling about this verdict and an analysis of the poem reinforces this uneasiness with the literal reading. The opening claim to be an inspired priest of song beginning his ceremony is unduly drawn out, unless we can read it in the tone of *Lambkin's Remains* ('Begin and somewhat loudly sweep the string'). And there are hints which lead us to this conclusion.

> Sacra facit vates: sint ora faventia sacris,
> > et cadat ante meos icta iuvenca focos.
> serta Philiteis certet Romana corymbis,
> > et Cyrenaeas urna ministret aquas.
> costum molle date et blandi mihi turis honores,
> > terque focum circa laneus orbis eat.
> spargite me lymphis, carmenque recentibus aris
> > tibia mygdoniis libet eburna cadis.
> ite procul fraudes, alio sint aere noxae:
> > pura novum vati laurea mollit iter.
> Musa, Palatini referemus Apollinis aedem:
> > res est, Calliope, digna favore tuo.   (1–12)

> *The bard begins the rites: let all voices be properly hushed for the rites, and let a heifer fall before my hearth. Let a Roman wreath challenge the ivy garland of Philitas and let a (Roman) urn dispense Callimachean water. Bring on soft spikenard and the glories of pleasing incense, and let a woollen circle go three times around the hearth. Sprinkle me with water and let the ivory flute pour fourth a libation of song from Phrygian jars on this new altar. Get ye far hence, all deceptions, and let all guilt remove to a different sky: the purifying*

---

29 Cf. pp. 42, 71 above. For a persuasive contrary view, see W.R. Johnson, 'The emotions of patriotism: Propertius 4.6', *California Studies in Classical Antiquity* 6 (1973) 151–80.

> *laurel branch gently prepares a new road for the bard.*
> *O Muse, we will tell of the house of Palatine Apollo: the*
> *subject, O Calliope, is worthy of your favour.*

In lines 3–4, Propertius implies again that he is the Roman
Callimachus, 'and to imperial order', which is his new road
(*novum . . . iter,* line 10) – but such grandiose beginnings have
been found in poems that turn out to be *recusationes* (cp. 3.3).
But we know from the opening elegy of Book 4 that Propertius
has disavowed, through Horos, all such claims. We would therefore expect him either not to write such a poem or to suppress
it if it was written earlier, or, on the view I am putting forward,
to write only a near parody of such a poem. This would make
it the climax of Propertius' *recusatio,* the defiant proof of Propertius' inability to write the sort of poetry Horace and, latterly,
Vergil wrote more successfully. I am suggesting that neither
Propertius' heart nor his talents are engaged in this poem and
this is revealed locally in a number of ways.

To continue the analysis. Lines 13–14 are frigidly excessive,
except on the reading suggested above:

> Caesaris in nomen ducuntur carmina; Caesar
>   dum canitur, quaeso, Iuppiter ipse vaces!

> *Poetry is being written on Caesar's glory: while Caesar*
> *is the subject, Jupiter, please lend me even your ears!*

Two crudely alliterative lines which might remind one of Horace's serious flattery of Augustus in such odes as 3.5, where there
is another but more seemly juxtaposition of Jupiter and Caesar.
The picture of Apollo on Augustus' poop firing arrows has long
provoked amusement or dislike among readers – can it be meant
as a serious poetic stroke? The whole tone of his subsequent
speech is high-pitched and slightly absurd. My suggestion is
that this – like Triton and all the sea goddesses applauding
Octavian's victorious standards, like all the exaggerations of
the picture, like Octavian's spear immediately following the
god's arrows, each one of which sank ten ships (*una decem
vicit missa sagitta rates,* line 68) – is deliberate and ironic playfulness.

'Enough of this martial poetry', Propertius finally says (*bella
satis cecini,* line 69) and in a coda as unduly drawn out as the

opening, unless we accept it as playful, he pictures himself and
other poets drinking till dawn and composing poetry on (what
else?) imperial conquests. The whole thing reads like a parody
of court poetry, not least of such poems as Horace's ode on
Cleopatra, published probably seven years earlier, perhaps even
of the Actium section of the *Aeneid* (8.675ff.), which Propertius may have heard recited. If the above piece of unorthodoxy
is correct, then Propertius *was* 'tying blue ribbon in the tails of
Virgil and Horace' with a vengeance. Nothing that we know of
ancient parody as seen in, say, the *Appendix Virgiliana* or what
we read of Propertius' humour in Book 4 makes the view unten-
able. And if the above case is proved we are rid of some embarrassing personal and poetic aspects of this elegy in particular
and Book 4 in general.

The real heart of the book, then, is still love poetry and the
two most successful poems are those on Cynthia (7 and 8),
since I do not share the wide admiration for 11, the so-called
regina elegiarum, whose rhetoric and self-righteousness makes
it much more of a 'court poem' than the others.[30] Elegy 8 in
particular, which Pound called 'The Journey to Lanuvium', is a
masterpiece of the style Propertius had slowly developed in his
progress towards becoming the Roman Callimachus. It is a
supremely ironic and humorous account of Cynthia's discovery
of Propertius with two ladies of the town. It is the purest example of the *tone* which, as I shall argue, Propertius has been
developing during his poetic career and which constitutes one
of his greatest debts to Callimachus. It must therefore be reserved for later discussion, when we have seen more specifically
what Propertius finally discerned in Callimachus.

Leptotes *and* logopoeia

From the first book onwards, where traces are admittedly few,
there is an intermittent but continuous movement away from
the apparently serious, direct, and passionate poetry about

---

30 Its subject, Cornelia, was the daughter of Scribonia, who had
   been married for a short time to Octavian and was the mother
   of Octavian's daughter Julia. She was the wife of L. Aemilius
   Paullus Lepidus, suffect consul of 34 B.C. and censor in 22 B.C.
   Her brother was consul in 16 B.C.

Cynthia, modelled on Catullus and perhaps others, to an ironic and dispassionate mode, which sometimes makes itself felt as a cooler and more objective attitude to his mistress and his passion. Elegies 2.6, 12, 15, 19, 22, 29, 33; 3.5, 8, 14, 16 and 23 might be singled out as examples.[31] Such self-mocking touches as the idyllic description of Propertius in the countryside with Cynthia, away from the wicked city, where he will go hunting like a modern Hippolytus – hares and smaller game, of course, not lions and boars – are evidence of this growing control:

> ipse ego venabor: iam nunc me sacra Dianae
>   suscipere et Veneri ponere vota iuvat.
> incipiam captare feras et reddere pinu
>   cornua et audaces ipse movere canes.
> non tamen ut vastos ausim tentare leones
>   aut celer agrestes cominus ire sues.
> haec igitur mihi sit lepores audacia molles
>   excipere et stricto figere avem calamo.   (2.19.17–24)

This might be paraphrased as:

> *A-hunting we will go. Now I want to become a devotee of the Virgin Goddess and give up my devotion to the Goddess of Love. I'll become a wild-game hunter and hang up their horns on a pine tree and even run the adventurous hounds myself. On the other hand I wouldn't be bold enough to take on great big lions or run to grips with wild pigs. So I'll confine my thirst for adventure to easy-going jackrabbits and catching a bird or two with a limed twig.*

An important example is 4.7 *(Sunt aliquid manes)*. Clearly this does not have the humour and irony of 4.8, but it lacks also the note of passionate and helpless involvement that is usually sought for in the *Monobiblos* and occasionally later. There is a dispassionate objectivity that, granted all the differ-

---

31 For a discussion of various obvious passages supporting this and of the literature on Propertius' humour and irony, which is *one* way of manifesting this tone, see E. Lefèvre, *Propertius Ludibundus: Elemente des Humors in seinen Elegien* (Heidelberg 1966).

ences of theme from 4.8, is yet reminiscent of it. After all, given what we know from the earlier books about Cynthia's relationship with Propertius, her cry 'I kept faith' (*me servasse fidem*, line 53) rings rather hollow. The ending, where, after her argumentative complaints, her ghost slips from Propertius' clasp:

> haec postquam querula mecum sub lite peregit,
>   inter complexus excidit umbra meos   (95–6),

seems deliberately nonchalant. The poem in fact seems a perfect balance between the usually 'serious' tone of the *Monobiblos* and the tone that Propertius gradually developed. To understand the tone, language and poetic style of Propertius, to understand the effects he was gradually trying to achieve, we must tread the dangerous path of using modern poetic analogies. Callimachus' and Propertius' *leptotes* is best explained in terms of verbal sophistication, what Ezra Pound called *logopoeia*.

In *How to Read* Pound distinguished between three kinds or 'manners' of poetry:

Melopoeia, 'wherein the words are charged, over and above their plain meaning, with some musical property, which directs the bearing or trend of the meaning';

Phanopoeia, 'which is a casting of images upon the visual imagination'; and

Logopoeia, 'the dance of the intellect upon words'. Of this Pound says:

> 'it employs words not only for their meaning, but it takes account in a special way of habits of usage, of the context we *expect* to find with the word, its usual concomitants, of its known acceptances, and of ironical play. It holds the aesthetic content which is particularly the domain of verbal manifestation, and cannot possibly be contained in plastic or in music. It is the latest come, and perhaps the most tricky and undependable mode.'[32]

Pound, in fact, believed that he had found this *logopoeia* in

32 See *Literary Essays of Ezra Pound* (ed.) T.S. Eliot (London 1954) 25.

Propertius: '. . . sometime after his first "book" S.P. ceased to be the dupe of magniloquence and began to touch words somewhat as Laforgue did'.[33]

It is important to understand exactly what Pound means by *logopoeia* before the case is considered for something analogous to it in Propertius. 'The dance of the intellect among words' is not, however, an illuminating description, since it might apply to metaphysical wit or puns; but some light is shed upon the concept in another essay – 'Irony, Laforgue and Some Satire'.[34]

> 'I do not think one can too carefully discriminate between Laforgue's tone and that of his contemporary French satirists. He is the finest wrought; he is the most "verbalist." Bad verbalism is rhetoric, or the use of *cliché* unconsciously, or a mere playing with phrases. But there is good verbalism, distinct from lyricism or imagism, and in this Laforgue is a master. He writes not the popular language of any country but an international tongue common to the excessively cultivated, and to those more or less familiar with French literature of the first three-fourths of the nineteenth century.'

And elsewhere he says of *logopoeia*

> '. . . you take the greater risk of using the word in some special relation to "usage," that is, to the kind of context in which the reader expects, or is accustomed, to find it.
>
> This is the last means to develop, it can only be used by the sophisticated.
>
> (If you want really to understand what I am talking about you will have to read, ultimately, Propertius and Jules Laforgue.)'[35]

What should be clear from this, as well as from other examples, such as Dorset, Rochester, Heine, and satirists in general, is that *logopoeia* is not, as one might immediately think, simply 'wit' of the Augustan or even metaphysical kind (even though

33 *The Letters of Ezra Pound* (ed.) D.D. Paige (New York 1950; London 1951) 245–6.
34 *Literary Essays of Ezra Pound*, 33.
35 *Ibid.* pp. 280 ff.

Rochester is in the direct line of the metaphysical tradition).
Nor is it the sort of verbal ambiguity analysed by William
Empson or the very rhetorical 'wit' we normally associate with
Tacitus. It is something more subtle than these. It is much more
a self-conscious poetic and ironic attitude which is expressed
through a certain way of writing. The clue is provided by Eliot
in the preface to the *Selected Poems,* although critics have not
generally made any use of it to unravel the term *logopoeia.*
Eliot says of the *Homage:*

> 'It is also a criticism of Propertius, a criticism which in
> a most interesting way insists upon an element of hu-
> mour, of irony and mockery, in Propertius, which
> Mackail and other interpreters have missed. I think that
> Pound is critically right, and that Propertius was more
> civilized than most of his interpreters have admitted. . .'

I suggest then that *logopoeia* is a refined mode of irony which
shows itself in certain delicate linguistic ways, in a sensitivity
to how language is used in other contexts, and in a deployment
of these other uses for its own humorous or satiric or poetic
aims, to produce an effect directly contrary to their effect in the
usual contexts. Thus magniloquence can be deployed *against*
magniloquence (*os magna sonaturum,* Hor. *Sat.* 1.4.43–4); allusions to other poets can be distorted from their original intent;
humility converted into confidence. *Logopoeia* is not simply
parody, for it may even be directed against the poet himself,
but a very self-conscious use of words and tone which would be
requisite for parody. Despite its sporadic appearance in other
periods it must strike us as an extremely 'modern' style of writing – which may explain why Pound thought that it was the
latest come and the most tricky to handle. Certainly there are
periods (the Homeric period, for example) in which it would
be utterly impossible as a poetic style, because the sensibility
which underlies it would be unthinkable; even Shakespeare
shows no trace of *logopoeia.* We of course are familiar with it:
the influence of Laforgue on Pound and Eliot has even affected
our critical view of some earlier poets in whom *logopoeia* is to
be found. As a result Rochester is now for us a modern in a
way Pope is not, and Propertius more modern than Vergil.

This abstract explanation may be better clarified by examples from the poets Pound cites, although it should be remembered that Pound is not a systematic critic and it is therefore quite likely that other poets could be produced who show distinct traces of the same quality.

For the English reader more recognizable examples of *logopoeia* are to be found in Eliot. It is unmistakably there in the use of conversational clichés and stock attitudes in 'Portrait of a Lady':

> Now that lilacs are in bloom
> She has a bowl of lilacs in her room
> And twists one in her fingers while she talks.
> 'Ah, my friend, you do not know, you do not know
> What life is, you who hold it in your hands';
> (Slowly twisting the lilac stalks)
> 'You let it flow from you, you let it flow,
> And youth is cruel, and has no remorse
> And smiles at situations which it cannot see.'
> I smile, of course,
> And go on drinking tea.

The Waste Land uses the technique in a more literary way:

> When lovely woman stoops to folly and
> Paces about her room again, alone,
> She smoothes her hair with automatic hand,
> And puts a record on the gramophone.

What then are the features in Propertius which would lead us to attribute to him, particularly in his later work, something of this poetic quality?

This question brings us, finally, to elegy 4.8. The poem is a minor masterpiece, carefully constructed, and here at least Propertius is in full control of his poetic effects. In a very subtle way, Propertius recapitulates many of the earlier themes of his poetry, as well as humorously half-keeping the promise of 4.1.69. In a typical fashion, familiar to us from Book 1, Propertius opens dramatically:

> Disce, quid Esquilias hac nocte fugarit aquosas,
>   cum vicina novis turba cucurrit agris;

turpis in arcana sonuit cum rixa taberna,
  si sine me, famae non sine labe meae. (1–2, 19–20)

Let me tell you what panicked the watery Esquiline last
night, when a whole crowd of neighbours scurried
around the new estates; when an unseemly row could
be heard in an out-of-the-way tavern – if without me,
not without damage to my reputation.

Propertius now gives an account of a festival at Lanuvium, a
town fifteen miles from Rome on the Via Appia. Cynthia, we
will learn, plans to attend it.

Lanuvium annosi vetus est tutela draconis;
  sicubi, tam rarae non perit hora morae;
qua sacer abripitur caeco descensus hiatu,
  qua penetrat (virgo, tale iter omne cave!)
ieiuni serpentis honos, cum pabula poscit
  annua et ex ima sibila torquet humo.
talia demissae pallent ad sacra puellae,
  cum temere anguino creditur ore manus.
ille sibi admotas a virgine corripit escas:
  virginis in palmis ipsa canistra tremunt.
si fuerint castae, redeunt in colla parentum,
  clamantque agricolae 'Fertilis annus erit.' (3–14)

Ancient Lanuvium is the custodian of an age-old snake;
here, if anywhere, an hour spent on such a rare sight
is not wasted. A sacred path descends steeply to the
sacred cavern with its black yawning mouth, through
which (virgins, avoid all such paths!) is sent the offering
to the starving serpent, when it demands its annual food
and hurls hisses from the lowest depths. The girls sent
down there grow pale at such a ceremony, when their
hands are rashly confided to the snaky jaws. It snatches
the tidbits if offered to it by virgins: (but even) in a
virgin's hands the very baskets tremble. If they have
been chaste, they return to the embrace of their parents
and the farmers cry out: 'It will be an abundant year!'

Propertius thus strikes the Callimachean note in two ways, first,
aetiologically, by the extended description of the agricultural

festival, and secondly, by the ironic thrusts at the expense of the virgins who participate in it. (Line 6 seems to have puzzled commentators, but it surely means that virgins should normally avoid such dark places, if they wish to remain so.) Propertius now brings in the personal element, but there is less melodrama and more cynicism in his jealousy here than in earlier books.

> huc mea detonsis avecta est Cynthia mannis:
>> causa fuit Iuno, sed mage causa Venus.
> Appia, dic quaeso, quantum te teste triumphum
>> egerit effusis per tua saxa rotis!
> spectaclum ipsa sedens primo temone pependit,
>> ausa per impuros frena movere locos.
> serica nam taceo vulsi carpenta nepotis
>> atque armillatos colla Molossa canes;
> qui dabit immundae venalia fata saginae,
>> vincet ubi erasas barba pudenda genas.
> cum fieret nostro totiens iniuria lecto,
>> mutato volui castra movere toro.   (15–28)

> *Hither my love Cynthia drove (in a carriage) with cropped ponies; the reason (given) was Juno, but the (real) reason was more likely Venus. Tell me, Appian Road, in what great triumph did she parade, as you watched, her wheels dashing over your rocky tracks! A great sight to see, with her leaning forward from her seat right over the yoke-pole, flapping the reins boldly over the rough places. Of course, I say nothing of the silky carriage of that depilated aristocrat and the Molossian hounds with the shiny collars around their necks – he'll be risking his life for a gladiator's pay and his filthy porridge and there the shaming beard will overrun those cleanshaven cheeks. Since so many insults were being inflicted on my bed, I wanted to change my place to sleep and move camp.*

Apart from the compressed (and almost untranslatable) wit, Propertius reintroduces the themes of Cynthia's infidelity and taste for luxury. This is almost the praetor from Illyria (2.16) reincarnated (compare even the typically pointed compressions in *maxima praeda tibi, maxima cura mihi* and *causa fuit Iuno, sed mage causa Venus*). Propertius curses them both in similar terms. Also noticeable are the military metaphors applied, as often, to the poet's love relationship with Cynthia and to Cynthia herself, the triumph, the spectacle and the moving of camps.[36] The difference, however, between this and similar elegies on his jealousy is the impression left upon us of distance and control.

Propertius now describes the girls he has decided to invite over to avenge himself for Cynthia's infidelity.

> Phyllis Aventinae quaedam est vicina Dianae;
>> sobria grata parum: cum bibit, omne decet.
> altera Tarpeios est inter Teia lucos;
>> candida, sed potae non satis unus erit.
> his ego constitui noctem lenire vocatis,
>> et Venere ignota furta novare mea.
> unus erat tribus in secreta lectulus herba.
>> quaeris concubitus? inter utramque fui.
> Lygdamus ad cyathos, vitrique aestiva supellex
>> et Methymnaei Graeca saliva meri.   (29–38)

There is a certain Phyllis who lives near (the temple of) Diana on the Aventine Hill – when sober, not too attractive: when she drinks, everything is right. The second, Teia, lives between the two Tarpeian groves; nice white skin, but in her cups one man won't be enough for her. I decided to invite them over to make the night more pleasant and return to my cheating ways with some loving I hadn't tried. One little couch was set up on a secluded lawn. Do you ask about the reclining arrangements? I was between the two of them. Lygdamus was butler; the service was the glass I use in summer; and the wine was Greek, a flavourful Methymnean.

36 A bolder example of playing on militaristic terms, pointed out by W.R. Nethercut, occurs at 2.1.36: *et sumpta et posita pace fidele caput*, where Propertius, in praising Maecenas' loyalty, plays on the Latin phrases for waging war (*arma/bellum sumere*) and surrendering (*arma ponere*), and so speaks audaciously of 'waging and surrendering peace'. The inversion 'wage peace' was later to be used by President Eisenhower during the Cold War.

Propertius goes on to describe the floral arrangements and the orchestra, as it were, but something is wrong. The atmosphere is ominous and he keeps losing at dice. In a wry and humorous echo of his earlier protestations of fidelity to Cynthia *(Cynthia prima fuit, Cynthia finis erit)*, he tells us that the two ladies of the town:

> cantabant surdo, nudabant pectora caeco:
>   Lanuvii ad portas, ei mihi, solus eram . . .   (47–8)

> *sang to my deaf ears, bared their breasts to my blind eyes: alas, I was not with them but at the gates of Lanuvium . . .*

The visual quality of Propertius' work is nowhere better illustrated than by the next scene:

> . . . cum subito rauci sonuerunt cardine postes,
>   et levia ad primos murmura facta Lares.
> nec mora, cum totas resupinat Cynthia valvas,
>   non operosa comis, sed furibunda decens.
> pocula mi digitos inter cecidere remissos,
>   palluerantque ipso labra soluta mero.
> fulminat illa oculis et quantum femina saevit,
>   spectaclum capta nec minus urbe fuit.
> Phyllidos iratos in vultum conicit ungues:
>   territa 'vicinae' Teia clamat 'aquam'.
> lumina sopitos turbant elata Quirites,
>   omnis et insana semita nocte sonat.
> illas direptisque comis tunicisque solutis
>   excipit obscurae prima taberna viae.
> Cynthia gaudet in exuviis victrixque recurrit
>   et mea perversa sauciat ora manu,
> imponitque notam collo morsuque cruentat,
>   praecipueque oculos, qui meruere, ferit.   (49–66)

> . . . *when suddenly the doors grated loudly on their hinges and there were low murmurs at the front of the house. Without any delay, Cynthia flings back wide the double doors; her hair was dishevelled, but she was still lovely in her anger. The cup dropped through my*

limp fingers and my drunken lips went white. She flashes lightning from her eyes and she rages as only a woman can, the spectacle was like a captured city. She jabs her angry nails into Phyllis' face: Teia, terrified, screams Fire! to the neighbourhood. Torches come out and alarm the slumbering citizenry and every street resounds with the nocturnal craziness. The first tavern in an obscure street takes the girls in, with their hair torn and their tunics unbelted. Cynthia exults over her spoils and runs back in victoriously; then she slashes my face with the back of her hand, imprints a great mark on my neck and bloodies it with her bite; she goes after my eyes especially, for they deserved it.

In this vivid and violent scene, characterized by the passion and physical fury we have encountered before (e.g. in 3.8), Propertius is still able to introduce his military metaphors, the captured city, the spoils, and the exultant conqueror, the Roman Boadicea. War should be confined to private life: this is the implication. The militaristic allusions are sustained to the end. Lygdamus, the servant heavily involved in his relationship with Cynthia (cf. 3.6; 4.7), is plucked from his hiding place, but Propertius is equally helpless:

> Lygdame, nil potui: tecum ego captus eram.
> supplicibus palmis tum demum ad foedera veni,
>   cum vix tangendos praebuit illa pedes,
> atque ait 'Admissae si vis me ignoscere culpae,
>   accipe, quae nostrae formula legis erit.' (70–4)

Lygdamus, I could do nothing: I was a captive like you. Then finally, with suppliant hands, I asked for her terms of truce, whereupon she grudgingly put out her feet to be touched. And she said: 'If you wish me to forgive this flagrant offence, here are the legal conditions I lay down'.

Propertius uses the appropriate language of military law in accepting her terms and the whole last section is clearly a parody of a conqueror imposing his peace terms on a defeated army.

Lygdamus, as part of Propertius' forces, is even to be sold on the slave market. The last line reinforces the extended metaphor:

respondi, et toto solvimus arma toro.   (88)

I was myself again, and we laid down our arms – all over the bed.

In fact, this humorous objectivity, which allows a lighter and more mocking treatment of Propertius' relations with Cynthia, has its counterparts elsewhere in the aetiological poems of Book 4. It is also impossible to imagine that such elegies as 2.22 and 33, and 3.6,8 and 23 as well as the very literary 4.5 are intended in the same spirit as the real love elegies. The long complaint about Isis, whose ceremonies are depriving Propertius of his usual pleasures, is quite absurd if meant as a serious poem: but the treatment indicates that there is a good deal of irony and literary humour intended. Similarly Propertius' susceptibility to women in general (2.22), his boasts of his amorous exploits and abilities, and his cynical conclusions are shockingly out of tone with the poems to Cynthia, unless we accept the presence in Propertius of some humour and some irony at his own expense. The defensiveness of the elegiac poet can show itself not only in a glorification of love as a subject but also in a certain self-depreciatory manner of writing, in an acknowledgment that he too knows what he is about and can take an objective view of his situation; he can in effect laugh at himself. It becomes a mannerism in Ovid, but in Propertius it seems a genuine attitude, albeit a precarious one. *Logopoeia* in the love poems then, or rather the Laforgian sensibility it expresses, is to be found in the interrelation of the serious poems to Cynthia and the occasional ironic reflections on Propertius' whole affair with Cynthia: the literary, military and mythological elements are indiscriminately at the service of either.

I conclude then that Propertius adapted from the Callimachean tradition not only his refusal to practice certain genres, to eschew certain topics, but also the appropriate *style* in which to treat his chosen themes. This is not to denigrate his originality nor even the debt he owed to the Latin tradition of personal erotic elegy: it is to assert why he could rightfully claim the title of 'Roman Callimachus'.

EPILOGUE

I have tried in this book to present a coherent picture of Propertius as a poet; I have tried to set him in his historical context and in the literary tradition in which he worked; and I have tried to produce a consistent account of his development, not simply chronologically, but also in terms of the *oeuvre* as it survives in our current texts. Psychohistory may be anathema to some, but I have invoked that particular discipline to clarify the long-disputed question of his relationship with Cynthia. My thesis is tolerably simple: Propertius did not deviate significantly from the earlier attitudes which he displayed in the *Monobiblos*; he simply refined them because of the usual ideological pressures which every Augustan poet felt. Few ancient poets, except Aeschylus, were heroes. However we take Horace's admission of throwing away his shield at Philippi, it must surely be interpreted as a symbolic resignation to a less than heroic posture on that field of battle. Propertius was not a hero either: he worked through, as best he could, his psychological problems and through his political differences with the Augustan regime. Influenced by the immediately preceding generation of Roman poets, the Neoterics, and influenced by the tradition of Callimachus, he became more and more deeply involved in that particular literary debate. His way of viewing matters literary was, coincidentally, entangled with certain ways of regarding the Roman Empire and its supreme leader Augustus: this, of course, was a problem which admitted of no easy solution. How he grappled with it is part, and an important part, of our assessment of his work. The traditional view sees Propertius as moving from a self-centered poetry of love to a disillusionment with that love, until he finally succumbs to Augustan pressures and in Book 4 makes an effort.

159

successful in some eyes, unsuccessful in others, to accept the Augustan demands and fulfil them in his own way without relinquishing his earlier Callimachean principles. This, I have suggested, is a falsification of Propertius' poetic development. The various strands of his poetry: the relationship with Cynthia; the steadfast adherence to Callimachean principles; his rejection of Augustan imperialism and the *mores* of the merchant, the soldier and the courtier; and, finally, his attitude to Augustan poetry, as typified by Horace, Vergil and others, are all inextricably interwoven, as one might expect from a poet of his complexity. He devised subtler techniques of self-expression, whether to depict more objectively his long and troubled relationship with Cynthia or to elude the demands of the time he lived in. Cynthia and Callimachus were his protection against public pressures, and art became his protection against Cynthia. In whatever vein he wrote, he was confident, beneath all the conventional elegiac postures of modesty, that future ages would understand the nature of his poetry and that his genius would stand the test:

> at non ingenio quaesitum nomen ab aevo
> excidet: ingenio stat sine morte decus.

SELECT BIBLIOGRAPHY

An almost full bibliography has now been provided by Hermann Harrauer, *A Bibliography to Propertius* (Hildesheim 1973). The following lists the works cited in the notes to this book and the articles, books and dissertations which I have found useful or interesting.

Abel, W. *Die Anredeformen bei den römischen Elegikern: Untersuchungen zur elegischen Form* (Diss. Berlin 1930).

Alfonsi, L. *L'elegia di Properzio* (Milan 1945).

Alfonsi, L. 'La donna dell'elegia latina', in *Ut pictura poesis: Studia latina P. J. Enk oblata* (Leiden 1955) 35–44.

Allen, A.W. 'Mythological examples in Propertius', *TAPA* 70 (1939) 28–9.

Allen, A.W. ' "Sincerity" and the Roman elegists', *CP* 45 (1950) 145–60.

Allen, A.W. 'Elegy and the classical attitude toward love, Prop. I. 1', *YCS* 2 (1950) 253–77.

Allen, A.W. '*Sunt qui Propertium malint*', in *Critical Essays on Roman Literature* (ed.) J.P. Sullivan (London 1962) 107–48.

Axelson, B. *Unpoetische Wörter* (Lund 1945).

Axelson, B. 'Der Mechanismus des ovidischen Pentameterschlusses', in *Ovidiana* (ed.) N.I. Herescu (Paris 1958) 121–35.

Baker, R.J. 'Miles annosus: the military motif in Propertius', *Latomus* 27 (1968) 322–49.

Baker, R.J. 'Propertius' lost bona', *AJP* 90 (1969) 333–7.

Baker, R.J. '*Laus in amore mori*: love and death in Propertius', *Latomus* 29 (1970) 670–98.

Barber, E.A. *Sexti Properti Carmina*[2] (Oxford 1960).

Bardon, H. *La Littérature latine inconnue* II (Paris 1956) 11–77.

Benda, J. *Properce, ou les amants de Tibur* (Paris 1928).

Boucher, J.-P. 'Le second livre de Properce', *REL* 41 (1963) 101–6

Boucher, J.-P. *Etudes sur Properce: Problèmes d'inspiration et d'art* (Paris 1965).

Boyancé, P. 'Properce', in *L'influence grecque sur la poésie latine de Catulle à Ovide: Entretiens Fond. Hardt II* (Geneva 1956) 169–222.

Brink, C.O. *Horace on Poetry, Prolegomena to the Literary Epistles* (Cambridge 1963).

Brooks, O. 'Propertius' Single Book', *HSCP* 70 (1965) 1–44.

Burck, E. 'Römische Wesenszüge der augusteischen Liebeselegie', *H* 80 (1952) 163–200.

Burck, E. 'Abschied von der Liebesdichtung', *H* 87 (1959) 191–211.

Butler, H.E. *Sex. Propertii Opera Omnia* (London 1905).

Butler, H.E. and Barber, E.A. *The Elegies of Propertius, Edited and with an Introduction and Commentary* (Oxford 1933).

Camps, W.A. *Propertius Elegies: Book I* (Cambridge 1961); *Book II* (1967); *Book III* (1966); *Book IV* (1965).

Cherniss, H. 'Biographical fashion in literary criticism', *U. of Cal. Publications in Class. Phil.* 12 (1943) 279ff.

Clausen, W.V. 'Callimachus and Roman poetry', *GRBS* 5 (1965) 193ff.

Commager, S. *The Odes of Horace* (New Haven/London 1962).

Copley, F.O. *Exclusus Amator. A Study in Latin Love Poetry* (Michigan–Oxford 1956).

Courtney, E. 'Three Poems of Propertius', *BICS* 16 (1969) 80–7.

Courtney, E. 'The structure of Propertius' Book III', *Phoenix* 24 (1970) 48–53.

Curran, L.C. 'Vision and reality in Propertius I 3', *YCS* 19 (1966) 187–207.

Damon, P.W. and Helmbold, W.C. *The Structure of Propertius Book 2, U. of Cal. Publications in Class. Phil.* 14 (1952).

D'Elia, S. 'Properzio e Orazio', *Annali della Facoltà di Lettere e Filosofia, Università di Napoli* 2 (1952) 45–77.

Diehl, E. *Pompeianische Wandinschriften* (Berlin 1930).

Dornseiff, F. 'Horaz und Properz', *Philologus* 87 (1932) 473–6.

Edwards, M.W. 'Intensification of meaning in Propertius and others', *TAPA* 92 (1961) 128–44.

Eisenhut, W. '*Deducere carmen*: Ein Beitrag zum Problem der literarischen Beziehungen zwischen Horaz and Properz', in *Gedankschrift für G. Rohde* (Tübingen 1961) 91–104.

Eliot, T.S. (ed.) *Literary Essays of Ezra Pound* (London 1954).

Enk, P.J. *Sex. Propertii elegiarum liber I (Monobiblos)* (Leiden 1946).

Enk, P.J. *Sex. Propertii elegiarum liber II* (Leiden 1962).

Fedeli, P. *Properzio: Elegie, libro IV, testo crit. e comm.* (Bari 1965).

Flach, D. *Das literarische Verhältnis von Horaz and Properz* (Giessen 1967).

Fontenrose, J. 'Propertius and the Roman career', *U. of Calif. Publications in Class. Philol.* 13 (1949) 371–88.

Fraenkel, E. *Horace* (Oxford 1957).

Freud, S. 'The most prevalent form of degradation in erotic life', in *Collected Papers* IV (London 1953) 203–16.

Freud, S. 'A special type of choice of object made by men', in *Collected Papers* IV (London 1953) 192–202.

Galinsky, K. 'The triumph theme in Augustan elegy', *WS* 3 (1969) 75–107.

Giardina, G.C. 'Orazio e Properzio: A proposito di Orazio, *Epist.* 2, 291 sqq', *RFIC* (1965) 24–40.

Goold, G.P. 'Noctes Propertianae', *HSCP* 71 (1966) 59–106.

Gow, A.S.F. and Page, D.L. (edd.) *The Greek Anthology: Hellenistic Epigrams* (Cambridge 1965).

Gow, A.S.F. and Page, D.L. (edd.) *The Greek Anthology: The Garland of Philip* (Cambridge 1968).

Green, P. 'Venus Clerke Ovyde', in *Essays in Antiquity* (London 1960) 109–35.

Grimal, P. *Les intentions de Properce et la composition du livre IV des Elégies* (Brussels 1953).

Hallett, J.P. *Book IV: Propertius' Recusatio to Augustus and Augustan Ideals* (diss. Harvard 1971).

Hallett, J.P. 'The role of women in Roman elegy: counter-cultural feminism', *Arethusa* 6 (1973) 103–20.

Helm, R. 'Sextus Propertius', *RE* 27 (1957) 758–96.

Highet, G. *Poets in a Landscape* (Pelican Books 1959).

Hubaux, J. 'Parthenius, Gallus, Virgile, Properce', in *Miscellanea Properziana* (Assisi 1957).

Humphries, A.R. *The Augustan World, Life and Letters in Eighteenth-Century England* (London 1964).

Jacoby, F. 'Zur Entstehung der römischen Elegie', *RhM* 60 (1905) 38–105.

Johnson, W.R. 'The emotions of patriotism: Propertius 4.6', *California Studies in Classical Antiquity* 6 (1973) 151–80.

Juhnke, H. 'Zum Aufbau des zweiten und dritten Buches des Properz', *H* 99 (1971) 91–125.

Klein, T.M. 'The role of Callimachus in the development of the concept of the counter-genre', *Latomus* 33 (1974) 217–31.

Lachmann, K. *Sexti Aurelii Propertii Carmina* (Leipzig 1816).

La Penna, A. *Properzio* (Florence 1951).

Lee, A.G. 'The date of Lygdamus and his relation to Ovidius', *PCPhS* 5 (1958/9) 15–22.

Lefèvre, E. *Propertius Ludibundus: Elemente des Humors in seinen Elegien* (Heidelberg 1966).

Lesky, A. *A History of Greek Literature* (London 1966).

Lewis, C.S. *The Allegory of Love* (Oxford 1936).

Lieberg, G. 'Die Mythologie des Properz in der Forschung und die Idealisierung Cynthias', *RhM* 112 (1969) 311–47.

Lilja, S. *The Roman Elegists' Attitude to Women* (Helsinki 1965).

Luck, G. *Die römische Liebeselegie* (Heidelberg 1961).

Luck, G. *The Latin Love Elegy* (London 1969).

Lucot, R. 'Problèmes de création chez Properce', *Pallas* 10 (1961) 59–68.

Ludwig, W. 'Zu Horaz, C. 2.1–12', *H* 85 (1957) 336–45.

Marcellino, R. 'Propertius and Horace: *Quis multa gracilis*', *CJ* 50 (1954–5) 321–5.

Marx, A. *De Sex. Propertii vita et librorum ordine temporibusque* (diss. Leipzig 1884).

Michels, A.K. 'Death and two poets', *TAPA* 86 (1955) 160–79.

Musurillo, H. *Symbol and Myth in Ancient Poetry* (New York 1961).

Nethercut, W.R. '*ille parum cauti pectoris egit opus*', *TAPA* 92 (1961) 389–407.

Nethercut, W.R. *Propertius and Augustus* (diss. Columbia, New York 1963).

Nethercut, W.R. 'Notes on the structure of Propertius' Book IV', *AJP* 89 (1968) 449–64.

Nethercut, W.R. 'The astrological significance of Propertius IV.1.150', *WS* 83 (1970) 110–17.

Nethercut, W.R. 'The ironic priest, Propertius' Roman Elegies', *AJP* (1970) 385–407.

Nethercut, W.R. 'Propertius, 3.11', *TAPA* 102 (1971) 411–43.

Newman, J.K. *Augustus and the New Poetry* (Brussels 1967).

Newman, J.K. *The Concept of Vates in Augustan Poetry, Collection Latomus* 89 (Brussels 1967).

Otis, B. 'Horace and the elegists', *TAPA* 76 (1945) 177–90.

Paige, D.D. (ed.) *The Letters of Ezra Pound* (New York 1950; London 1951).

Paratore, E. *L'Elegia III, 11 e gli Atteggiamenti politici di Properzio* (Palermo 1936).

Pfeiffer, R. *Callimachus*: Vol. I *Fragmenta*[2] (Oxford 1965); Vol. II *Hymni et Epigrammata* (1952).

Pfeiffer, R. *History of Classical Scholarship* (Oxford 1968).

Pillinger, H.E. 'Some Callimachean influences on Propertius, Book 4', *HSCP* 73 (1969) 171–99.

Platnauer, M. *Latin Elegiac Verse* (Cambridge 1951).

Plessis, F. *Etudes critiques sur Properce et ses élégies* (Paris 1884).

Rankin, A.V. '*Odi et Amo*,' *American Imago* 17 (1960) 437–48.

Reitzenstein, E. *Wirklichkeitsbild und Gefühlsentwicklung bei Properz* (*Philologus Suppltbd.* 29.2, Leipzig 1936).

Ross, D.O., Jr. *Style and Tradition in Catullus* (Cambridge, Mass. 1969).

Rostagni, A. 'L'influenza greca sulla origini dell'elegia erotica latina', in *L'influence grecque sur la poésie latine de Catulle à Ovide. Entretiens Fond. Hardt. II* (Geneva 1956) 59–92.

Rothenstein, M. *Die Elegien des Sextus Propertius* (Berlin 1898).

Saylor, C.F. *Propertius and the Main Themes of Roman Amatory Thought* (diss. Berkeley 1968).

Schmeisser, B. *A Concordance to Propertius* (Hildesheim 1972).

Sellar, W.Y. *The Roman Poets of the Augustan Age: Horace and the Elegiac Poets* (Oxford 1899).

Shackleton Bailey, D.S. *Propertiana* (Cambridge 1956).

Skutsch, O. 'The structure of the Propertian *Monobiblos*', *CP* 58 (1963) 238–9.

Slater, P. *The Glory of Hera* (Boston 1968, 1971).

Smyth, W.R. *Thesaurus criticus ad Sexti Propertii textum* (Leiden 1970).

Solmsen, F. 'Propertius and Horace', *CP* 43 (1948) 105–9.

Sullivan, J.P. 'Two problems of Roman love elegy', *TAPA* 92 (1961) 522–8.

Sullivan, J.P. '*Castas odisse puellas*: a reconsideration of Propertius 1.1', *WS* 74 (1961) 92–112.

Sullivan, J.P. *Ezra Pound and Sextus Propertius: A Study in Creative Translation* (Austin, Texas 1964; London 1965).

Syme, R. *The Roman Revolution* (Oxford 1939, 1960).

Terzaghi, N. 'Orazio e Properzio', in *Studia Graeca et Latina* (Turin 1963) 1174–96.

Tomaszuk, P.V. *A Romantic Interpretation of Propertius: Vincenzo Padula* (Aquila 1971).

Tränkle, H. *Die Sprachkunst des Properz und die Tradition der lateinischen Dichtersprache, Hermes Einzelschr.* 15 (Wiesbaden 1960).

van Groningen, B.A. *La poésie verbale grecque* (Amsterdam 1953).

Webster, T.B.L. *Hellenistic Poetry and Art* (London 1964).

Wheeler, A.L. 'Propertius as Praeceptor Amoris', *CP* 5 (1910) 28–40.

Wight Duff, J. *A Literary History of Rome, From the Origins to the Close of the Golden Age*² (London 1960).

Wili, W. 'Die literarischen Beziehungen des Properz zu Horaz', in *Festschrift für E. Tièche* (Bern 1947) 179–90.

Wilkins, E.H. *The Making of the 'Canzoniere' and Other Petrarchan Studies* (Rome 1951).

Williams, G. 'Some aspects of Roman marriage', JRS 48 (1958) 16–29.

Williams, G. *Tradition and Originality in Roman Poetry* (Oxford 1968).

Wimmel, W. *Kallimachos in Rom: Die Nachfolge seines apologetischen Dichtens in der Augusteerzeit, Hermes Einzelschr.* 16 (Wiesbaden 1960).

INDEX OF PROPERTIAN PASSAGES

167

GENERAL INDEX

Accius, 68
Actium, battle of, 42, 58, 60, 65,
    71–2, 77, 135, 144, 147
addressees (of Propertian odes), 6;
    see also specific names
Aeneidomastix, 67
Aeschylus, 36, 159
aetiology, 41, 71–3, 111, 120, 134–8,
    144
Agrippa, 67
Alba, kings of, 37
Albius, *see* Tibullus
Alcaeus, 9n, 14, 26, 30, 69
Alexander Aetolus, 109
Alexandrians and Alexandrianism,
    9, 11, 19, 25, 31, 33–4, 36–7, 42,
    45–9, 51–2, 68–71, 73–6, 82, 101,
    108–14, 116–18, 120–2, 129–30,
    132–3, 136, 138; diction, 114–15;
    meaning of 'Alexandrian', 109;
    *see also specific genres and
    writers*
Allen, A. W., 76n, 94n, 108n
Alphesiboea, 105
Amor, 59, 89, 104–6; *see also* love
Anacreon, 31
Anthologia Graeca, 9n
Anthologia Palatina, 112n, 129n
Antimachus, 112–13, 133
Antonius, L., 1
Antonius, M., (Antony), 1–2, 23,
    79, 83, 118
Apollo, 37, 39, 41, 71, 78–9, 94,
    125–6, 134, 141–3, 145–6;
    inauguration of temple of, 7, 35
Apollonius Rhodius, 109–11, 113–15
Appendix Virgiliana, 147
Apuleius, 78–9
Arabia, expedition to, 58

Aratus, 109, 111, 113–14
Archias, 62
Arethusa, 41–2
Aristodemus of Nysa, 136
Aristophanes, 54, 110
Artemis, 79
Asclepiades of Samos, 109, 112, 119
Atalanta, 32, 101, 105–6
Athenaeus, 129n
Athens, 2, 66
auctoritas, 10
Auden, W. H., 129n
Augustus Caesar (formerly
    Octavian), 1–2, 9–10, 13, 15–16,
    22–4, 31, 33n, 34, 37–8, 40–2, 44,
    46n, 55, 57, 59–60, 62–4, 66,
    68, 70–1, 73–4, 120, 126, 146,
    147n, 159; *see also* politics, Rome
Ausonius, 47
Axelson, B., 69n, 129n

Bacchylides, 69
Bactria, 13, 58
Baehrens, E., 49
Baiae, 98
Barber, E. A., 51, 52n, 108
Bardon, H., 8n, 69n
Bassus, 3, 6, 9
Bastarnae, 43
Benda, J., 52, 107–8
Bentley, R., 79
Bion, 109
Borges, Jorge Luis, 55
Boucher, J.-P., 78n, 126n
Brink, C. O., 120n
Britain, expedition to, 41, 58
Burmann, P., the Younger, 49
Butler, H. E., 50, 52n, 108

168

O'Hara, J., 91
Omphale, 21
Otis, Brooks, 75n
Ovid, x, 2–3, 8, 10–11, 27, 29, 31,
   35, 40, 42, 45–8, 52, 60–1, 63–5,
   67–8, 71, 73–5, 78–9, 87–90, 101,
   108, 112n, 114, 117, 127–8, 129n,
   133, 136, 144, 158; *Amores*, 6, 25,
   46; *Ars Amatoria*, 32, 45–6, 64–5,
   67, 88; *Fasti*, 46, 52, 71; *Heroides*,
   41, 46; *Metamorphoses*, 45, 73–5,
   114; metre, 5; and Propertius,
   61, 63–5, 73–5; quoted, 61, 64–5,
   112; *Remedia Amoris*, 88

Pacuvius, 68
Padula, Vincenzo, 50; quoted, xiii
Paetus, 38
Paige, D. D., 53n, 150n
Palatine Anthology, 112n, 129n
paraclausithyron, 9, 33, 37, 129
Paratore, E., 21n
parody, 146–7, 151, 157
Parthenius of Nicaea, 68, 109, 113n,
   114, 118–19, 136
Parthians, 8, 14, 34, 37–8, 41–2, 55,
   58–9, 64
Pasiphae, 88, 133
Passenni family, 1; Passennus
   Paulus, 3, 46
pastoral poetry, 68
patronage, 9–10, 67–8; *see also*
   Maecenas, Messala
peace (as poetic theme), 14, 31,
   56, 59; *see also* war
Peripatetics, 120
Persephone, 4, 6
Persia, expedition to, 58
Persius, 2, 54, 112, 115, 130–1
Perusia, 1, 33n, 57, 66
Petrarch F., 48–9
Petronius, 47–8, 88, 108, 129n
Pfeiffer, R., 111n
phanopoeia, 149
Philippi, 57, 159
Philitas, 12, 15–16, 25, 36–7, 68, 70,
   109, 112, 113n, 114, 125–7, 134,
   145
Philodemus, 69
Phoenix of Colophon, 109
Pillinger, H. E., 41n
Pindar, 14, 30, 69, 110, 131

Pirithous, 30, 105
Platnauer, M., 127
Plato, 113, 117
Plautus, 110
Plessis, F., 76
Pliny, the Younger, 1, 3, 46, 113n
Plutarch, 38, 136
poetry, *see specific genres*
politics, Augustan, ix-x, 89, 159;
   and literature, 54–5, 65–70, 73–5;
   see also Rome
Pollio, Asinius, 68
Polybius, 63
Pompeii, 47, 81
Pompey, 22, 55, 68, 74
Ponticus, 3, 6, 9, 32, 126
Pope, Alexander, 109, 151
Poseidippus of Samos, 109, 112,
   119
Postumus, 38
Pound, Ezra, ix, 13–14, 24, 53, 109,
   114–16, 147, 149–52
Praxiphanes, 119
Prévost, Abbé A. F., 91
Proclus, 113n
Propertius: chronology of writings,
   3–8; and Cynthia, *see* Cynthia;
   diction and style, 116–17, 127–9,
   149–58; family, 1; history of
   Propertian studies, ix-x, 46–53;
   and Horace, 12–14, 17–21, 23–5,
   27–31, 37, 39, 55, 120–2; life, 1–2,
   45–6; literary environment, 8–11
   (*see also under* Rome); Monobiblos (Book 1), 3–6, 9, 30, 47,
   57, 97, 103, 105–6, 121, 127n, 149,
   159; and Ovid, 61, 63–5, 73–5;
   psychology, 93–106; Roman
   régime and empire, attitude to,
   13–14, 23, 37–8, 40–5, 51, 57–60,
   64, 70–3, 121, 159–60; themes,
   31–45, 53, 89–90, 122–6, 129–30
   (*see also* aetiology, mythology,
   recusatio)
Proust, M., 91
pseudonyms, 78–9
Ptolemy Philadelphus, 110
publication, forms of, in Rome, 8

Quintilian, 112n, 118–19, 129n;
   quoted, 47